4-11

CAPTIVE ON THE
HO CHI MINH TRAIL

by
MARJORIE A. CLARK

48472

MOODY PRESS
CHICAGO

Printed in the United States of America

FOREWORD

We have a prayer for you as you read this book. We pray that you will join us in praising the living God as you read how He cares for His children today. And we pray that your heart will respond with ours to the invitation of the Lord Jesus: "Take My yoke upon you, and learn of Me, for I am gentle and humble in heart; and you shall find rest for your souls" (Matthew 11:29, *New American Standard Bible*). In obedience to Christ, there are no regrets.

Mr. and Mrs. Leslie H. Chopard went to Laos in 1958. Initially they worked in Saravane, Laos. Later they moved further north to Savannakhet on the Mekong River near the seventeenth parallel. When they returned from furlough in 1965, they located in Kengkok, a town of two to three thousand people, thirty miles southeast of Savannakhet. They began to work, building up the church in Kengkok and itinerating in many surrounding villages, dispensing medicine and evangelizing. Literacy work, care of tuberculosis patients, and agricultural aid projects also were undertaken. There they worked until they went home for furlough in 1970.

Meanwhile the Lord was leading some young people to join them in His work in Laos. Beatrice Kosin, an experienced school teacher from Des Moines, Washington, became convinced the Lord would have her in Laos, particularly to work with children. Evelyn Anderson, a registered nurse from Coldwater, Michigan, had her heart set on serving the Lord in Laos as well. For some time she had carefully prepared to work in Laos by going to a Bible school, working in the emergency room of a city hospital, and attending a course in tropical medicine for missionaries in Toronto, Canada. Lloyd Oppel, from Courtenay, British Columbia, after one year at the University of British Columbia, was guided by the Lord to go to Laos. He planned to help with construction projects. I'm

3

Sam Mattix from Centralia, Washington. While still in high school, I became definitely interested in serving the Lord with the Chopards in Laos. In 1970-71 I went one year to community college, then when the Chopards went back to Laos in the fall of 1971 with Bea, Ev, and Lloyd, I went to London to attend a nine-month course at the Missionary School of Medicine. I got to Laos in July of 1972, seven months after the others had arrived.

Much could be written of the interesting experiences of each one of these new missionaries to Laos. The author is a friend of the Oppel family and has known Lloyd from childhood. With access to his letters home from Laos, she has been able to give a good picture of the life of the young missionary in Laos. The situaton is better visualized through the eyes of one person, Lloyd, than through the experiences of all of us put together.

This story would not have been written except for the events that began on October 28. In the early morning hours of that day, North Vietnamese soldiers moved into Kengkok and the surrounding villages. Lloyd and I were captured as we tried to escape. The Chopards were able to get to safety just ahead of the advancing troops. Bea Kosin and Evelyn Anderson's house was in the section of town first overrun by the troops. Because there was no opportunity for escape, they wisely hid under their beds in the house. Their story was later pieced together: after two days of hiding in their locked house, they were discovered by North Vietnamese soldiers. They were captured and held, while Lao Christians bargained valiantly for their release. For unknown reasons, the negotiations fell through, and the girls were executed by rifle, according to the report considered most reliable. When the Royal Lao Army retook the town of Kengkok later that week, the bodies of our two sisters in Christ were found in the smouldering ruins of a house across the street from their own. Bea and Ev gave their lives in the service of our Lord Jesus. We take comfort in the fact that they are now with the Lord. Because of this, Lloyd and I realize more than ever before that we are pilgrims on earth. Bea and Ev are no longer pilgrims—they have arrived at their home in the heavenly country. With them we say it is our desire: "that with all boldness, Christ shall even now, as always, be exalted in my body, whether by life or by death. For to me, to live is Christ, and to die is gain" (Philippians 1:20-21, *New American Standard Bible*).

SAM MATTIX

Lloyd Oppel arriving home in Vancouver, British Columbia.

Sam Mattix at McChord Air Force Base near Seattle.

1

The Lord is my shepherd (Psalm 23:1).

Lloyd Dudley Oppel was only nineteen years old—perhaps the youngest missionary in southeast Asia—when he went to Laos in late 1971 to become a practical helper and missionary-in-training under Mr. and Mrs. Les Chopard of Christian Missions in Many Lands. But into his life he had already crammed many experiences which would prove useful to him in his work, and he had learned many lessons which would stand him in good stead.

Most of his growing years were spent in Courtenay, a sleepy little town in central Vancouver Island. From childhood, Lloyd believed in participation, in throwing himself wholeheartedly into whatever he did. And he believed in laughter and singing and a little nonsense now and then. Taking the lead at junior high school in Oscar Wilde's *The Importance of Being Ernest,* he stood the house on its ears by being earnestly Ernest in the tongue-in-cheek way required of the comedy. But at times he could be serious too, and idealistic, and intense.

Because of reversals in business ventures and a breakdown in health, Lloyd's father was never able to keep the family in what is referred to as comfortable circumstances. They have never had much of this world's goods, but they are rich in their love and concern for others and deeply interested in God's work and workers.

The strength and stability of Christian life in the Oppel home comes from Lloyd's mother, Phyllis. She loves to read, study, and teach God's Word. Better still, she seeks to live by it. Her eyes, dark brown like Lloyd's, glow with warmth and light as she speaks of what Christ means to her. She has infused this

9

spirit into all her children, so that Lloyd's older brother is a Bible teacher and very active in Christian work. His sister Louise, as soon as she completed nurse's training, offered herself for missionary work in Nigeria, and Lloyd at an early age felt the tug of Christ's claims upon his life.

Partly because of financial pressures and partly because of their concern for deserted and neglected children, the Oppels became foster parents to several Indian babies, one of whom, now a junior miss, they still have. It may be that these foster babies in the home were part of God's plan in preparing Lloyd for Laos. Certainly they gave him a love for all children.

As well as financial troubles, the family experienced suffering and ill health. Lloyd was only twelve when it was found that his mother had cancer and major surgery was needed.

In spite of the lack of material blessings, in spite of what seems to be more than their share of troubles and difficulties, there was always joy and fun in the home. There was music and mimicry, lightness and laughter.

At Vanier Senior Secondary School, Lloyd identified himself with Inter School Christian Fellowship, becoming president of the group. ISCF sponsor, Albert Wedel, was also the school's choral director and music teacher. With his musical ability, his strong singing voice, and his guitar, Lloyd became active in the school's music program.

When asked what experiences proved most useful later in Laos, Lloyd replied without hesitation, "My years at Camp Imadene." Imadene is a Bible camp at Maple Bay on Vancouver Island. Here Lloyd went first as a camper and then as a worker. He spent four entire summers, as well as Easter vacations, at the camp as "general everything." He became dishwasher, boat builder and repairman, septic tank cleaner, painter, and carpenter as well as counselor, song leader, and preacher. In between camps, he had practical experience in camping out, spending a night here and there on the channel islands. At the camp he gained experience and self-confidence in practical areas, while the spiritual atmosphere built up his Christian life.

10

2

And the Spirit of God moved upon the face of the waters (Genesis 1:2).

In September 1970, Lloyd enrolled at the University of British Columbia in Vancouver. As yet he had no clear directive as to what he wanted to be, but he felt safe in starting with a general science course. At least he would find out what he was capable of handling. Biology interested him, and he decided to major in that field—certainly physics was not his forte! The idea of medicine began to appeal to him. He did not want to be a doctor, particularly, but what about becoming a professional nurse, a physiotherapist, or a pharmacist?

As far back as he could remember, he had had the desire of someday going to the mission field. He had read many missionary letters, listened to reports, seen endless slides. To him, it was almost as if a Christian should go unless the door were definitely closed. Since Louise had gone to Nigeria, all the family had become intensely interested in missionaries and their doings.

But as yet there was no leading, no moving of the Spirit, no light upon the way. Lloyd's Christianity was as general as his other studies. He was nominally interested in Christian music, study, and youth work, but nothing definite.

Then God's Spirit began to deal with his soul. Why was he there at the university? What did he expect to get out of it? Were these studies just to satisfy his ego, to take away his feeling of insecurity? Was he just trying to prove himself good at something? These things were not necessarily bad, but something was missing from his life. He realized that as a Christian, his total security must be in Christ and not in his own talents

11

or abilities. He must look to the Lord for specific direction, rather than giving his efforts to building a future for himself. His primary interest was still in the area of medicine, but a professional nursing course would take five years. Why not spend a year on a mission field somewhere to find what skill or training would serve him best? Would he be a better servant of the gospel and of the people if he had medical training first?

While his thoughts turned to the practical aspects of Christian witness, he also began to realize the necessity of spending time in prayer and studying the Word of God. Christ Himself became more real to him, his daily Christian experience more vital. He gobbled up the Scriptures, spent more time in prayer, and felt growing within him a need to reach out to others, especially those in distant areas. But he knew nothing of Laos or of the need of the people who lived there.

One day's mail brought a mimeographed circular from F. Irving Benton of Ontario with news and needs of the mission field. A headline caught Lloyd's eye: *Needed in Laos—People with Practical Skills.* Practical skills on the mission field! Wasn't that what he wanted, to find out what practical skills would be useful on the mission field and open doors to further Christian witness and service? Eagerly he read the report from Les Chopard in Kengkok, Laos. Workers were needed for building a Bible school and clinic.

Man, that's just what I want, Lloyd thought. While still at the university, he filled in an application for a passport and sent it off to Ottawa. As soon as school was out, he went to see Mr. and Mrs. Chopard, who were staying just south of the US-Canadian border. Then he headed home to Courtenay, where he asked the assembly of believers at Elim Gospel Chapel to commend him for work in Laos. By July, he was on his way down the coast to San Francisco and was scheduled to sail on the *SS Hawaii* to Bangkok on or about August 19 on his way to Laos.

Three other young people had been commended to work in Laos: Evelyn Anderson, a registered nurse and student of Emmaus Bible School; Beatrice Kosin, a school teacher; and Sam Mattix, who was first going to London for a special course in medicine. The girls and Lloyd were to sail with Mrs. Chopard.

Of conditions in Laos at this time, Les Chopard wrote, "We would be less than candid if we said that Laos wasn't in trouble. The political situation is as bad as it has ever been, and much of the Lord's work is threatened by opposing, invading forces."

There was trouble in Laos. But there was trouble in America too—trouble which hindered the hoped-for August sailing.

3

They encamped there by the waters (Exodus 15:27).

During a brief visit with the Chopards in the Seattle-Tacoma area, Lloyd was kept busy singing and speaking at gospel chapels, helping to pack, and studying to read and write the Lao language. "So far, so good," he wrote home. "I think it will be OK until I get to Laos and find I can't understand anyone!"

Labor conditions did not boost hopes for an early sailing. "Everything is fouled up. The longshoremen are out [on strike] —also all the construction workers. The nurses are threatening, and the railroad just went back to work," he wrote. Les Chopard was looking for a Toyota jeep which would be of invaluable help to the work on the field. In Laos there was a six-month waiting list; but things were not much better in the United States, and because of the longshoremen's strike, Japanese cars were as scarce as hen's teeth.

Now the long wait began. Lloyd traveled down to Oakland with the Chopards, where they found the missionary Home of Peace already full of missionaries waiting to sail, and the warehouse and yard packed with barrels, crates, generators, and radio equipment waiting to be shipped when the strike was over.

Because of crowded conditions at the Home of Peace, the Chopard party became the house guests of Dr. DaSheill of Oakland, who cared for several handicapped adults in a large and comfortable home.

Waiting time proved to be working time. First, there was shopping and packing useful items: soap, stationery, tapes, blankets, charts, mattresses, shoes, medicine, folding chairs, socks, mops, nails, screws, pitchfork, powdered salad dress-

14

ing, blinds, pictures, pumps, projector, typewriters, towel racks, flooring glue, washing machine, cutlery, crocks, and so forth.

For Lloyd, there was the continuing study of Lao, written on lined paper something like a musical score except there were six lines. The consonants and vowels themselves looked as if they were something to be played, but they represented sounds which he would have to learn.

Craving activity, Lloyd offered his services to Bethesda Home in the building of a hospital for elderly citizens. He was given the task of tearing cupboards out of the kitchen in an old house on the property. He found it so overrun with cockroaches that he had to keep a sharp eye on his tools, fearing they might disappear before his very eyes.

Carpentry work proved enjoyable. "I laid the plywood down on the floors in the kitchen, bathroom, and hallway," he wrote. "I guess the quality of workmanship here must not be too great 'cause everyone seems taken with the quality of my work! It's purely a fluke that all the joints came out so tight, but I'm keeping my mouth shut and soaking up the compliments. When they ask me where I learned such craftsmanship, I tell that my father was an artisan of many and diverse talents!"

The longshoremen's strike was in its eighty-eighth day with no sign of a break, so Lloyd continued work on the house, putting gyproc and paneling on the walls. Most of the work was volunteer, and his co-workers were "retired Christian types." The damage was not serious when Lloyd accidentally bashed one of them on the head with his hammer, but thereafter the willing worker always chose to wear a hat when he was in Lloyd's vicinity.

Two months of search failed to locate the desired Toyota jeep, but early in October, Mr. Chopard and Lloyd flew down to Los Angeles to look around. They found just what they were looking for, a red land cruiser with a white roof. They waited for special equipment to be installed and then climbed aboard for the trip back to Oakland. Lloyd saw his first oil wells and cotton fields, enjoyed fresh oranges, grapes, plums, and nectarines bought at wayside stands, and reveled in the beauty of the sequoia forest, bemoaning the fact that he had not brought his camera along. Forest scenes reminded him of his beloved island home and caused what he described as "a lump in my pump."

By October 10, the longshoremen had been sent back to work. The States Line informed the waiting missionaries that they hoped to sail by the end of the month. If they left by November 1, they should be in Bangkok around November 24 and in to Kengkok, Laos, around December 1. Now that there was hope for an early sailing, Les Chopard left for Bangkok by plane in order to make the necessary preparations for the arrival of the party. This left Lloyd to assume the responsibility of tying things up at the American end. He welcomed the activity, feeling that if he became any more anxious to get underway, he would surely burst!

First, there was work to be done on the Toyota to make it suitable for work in Laos. Then he applied himself to language study for three hours each morning under the tutelage of Mrs. Chopard. He would soon be literate in Lao—that is, able to read aloud and write—only he did not know what he was reading and writing.

Sailing date made big news—November 12, 1971. They were to arrive in Bangkok on December 2, exactly four months after the original sailing date. A week later, Lloyd wrote home, "They're monkeying around with our sailing date again. Nothing is sure." But now that ships were moving, it meant there was room at the warehouse of the States Line.

Crates had to be measured—all seventeen of them—to determine cubic footage. Then they were weighed, and full particulars were listed. Including the truck, total weight added up to fourteen thousand pounds. Lloyd worked eight to nine hours without a break, using a hand truck to move crates weighing five to seven hundred pounds. His only helper, a skinny wisp of a guy, tipped the scales at only 115 pounds. His letter describing these activities ended with a picture of himself as an open-mouthed sleeper in bed, and a long string of z-zs.

At last the visas were obtained, the crates loaded, the baggage packed. At two P.M. on November 8, Mrs. Chopard, Beatrice Kosin, Evelyn Anderson, and Lloyd boarded the vessel *Arizona* of the States Line.

They were aboard and afloat, but not away.

4

They that go down to the sea in ships, that do business in great waters (Psalm 107:23).

Lloyd's letter-diary recounts what happened once the group of missionaries were on board the ship.

November 8, 10:00 P.M. "We're still in port, they're still busy loading—haven't posted a departure time. We told the Christian folk if they wanted to say good-bye, they could drop out around 7:00. We expected about ten or fifteen, providing they could get security clearance, but about forty turned up. Wow! They brought flowers, candy, and presents, and we really had a good time. We watched them disappear down the dock, looked around at the military regalia, and realized afresh that we are soldiers and pilgrims. 'For here we have no permanent home, but we are seekers after the city which is to come.' "

November 9, 12:05 P.M. "We're still in port; the longshoremen work like snails, but we're supposed to sail in approximately an hour. After lunch we took a stroll down the pier to look at the *SS Michigan*. It's a palatial freighter compared to ours. The *Arizona* is nineteen years old and a rust-bucket.

"My roommate came aboard today and trust we'll make out, but he's got a few strikes against him. First, he's twice as big as I, so I can't smash him around. Second, he's an ex-Navy man, so we shan't see eye to eye politically. Third, he's a chain smoker, so I may die of bronchitis before we reach the Orient."

17

November 10, 1:48 A.M. "Set sail.

2:35 A.M. Last sight of land.

2:00 P.M. Very much at sea, both the ship and my stomach! Barf! Still in bed. The ocean is very rough, much water over the decks. Feel like Paul."

November 11. "Bad night for sailing, stuff flying around my room. Some water damage when my teapot fell over. Almost fell out of bed once or twice."

After Lloyd got his sea legs, life aboard the ship took on a more regular routine. He began to give Evelyn Anderson guitar lessons, and he worked on his stamp collection. In a few days the weather warmed enough for shorts and sun bathing. His roommate, Roger, the ex-Navy man headed for the Philippines for a vacation, proved easy to get along with after all.

The Christian group met daily at an early hour for reading and prayer. While they were having devotions one morning, the cabin boy Don, a sixty-one-year-old Filipino, came in to change the linen. It was prayer time, and Lloyd's head was bowed in his hands.

"Don't feel too unhappy, boy!" Don sympathized. "In seven more days we reach land!"

Ten people were at the first Sunday morning service held aboard the freighter when Lloyd did the preaching. He listed them as six sinners and four saints. Four sailors came and sat through the sermon with folded hands, pious looks, and occasional smirks. Lloyd's roommate, Roger, and Don the cabin boy, both stayed behind to ask questions.

To celebrate Mrs. Chopard's birthday, the ship's chef baked a special cake, complete with candles which could not be blown out. Fun gifts caused a great deal of amusement. Lloyd had carved a model ship from soap and rigged it with toothpicks, then fitted it into a glass—ship in a bottle, of course. Towels and face cloth, courtesy of the States Line, were presented with the note, "Monogrammed linens, from the last of the bigtime spenders." There was even a map of the ship because Mrs. Chopard was always getting lost.

That evening they talked for a long time with Roger and another passenger, both of whom were evidently searching for an answer to life's problems. But neither could seem to grasp the fact that they could be saved by grace, and not by works.

They arrived at Yokosuka, Japan, on November 22 and were able to go ashore, visiting Tokyo one day and Yokohama another. To Lloyd, they were similar in many ways to American cities.

Pusan, in Korea, was something else again. Their guide in Pusan was a university student.

"If I thought the traffic in Japan was something, here it is double something," Lloyd wrote. "Wow! Everyone sits on the horn continually. All the bicycles and cars have bells and klaxons and noise is phenomenal! Driving through the streets, the people and kids are like ants. The streets are narrow and full of buses and trucks and taxis and bicycles and carts and ponies and cars and cows and kids, ad infinitum. The shops are crowded, and the whole setting far more oriental than Japan, with men and women wearing traditional dress. They built a freeway in Pusan for a few miles, but nobody uses it like one because there are people and cows on it, just like the side streets. We went twenty miles out of the city to a very important, very old Buddhist temple in the hills. Through our guide, I asked a couple of old ladies if I could take their pictures, and they consented. They stood looking very grave until the picture was taken, and then giggled and giggled and bowed and went through the whole routine!"

Always attracted to children, Lloyd found the children in Korea were also attracted to him and followed him around. He took pictures, let them look through the viewfinder of the camera and listen to his watch.

As the group walked along the beach in the evening dusk, they passed several stalls where seafood was sold.

"One old granny was selling some spiny effort that looked like a rubber anemone," he wrote, "so I said I'd try one. She cut it open and pulled out the inside, dipped it in hot sauce and—down the hatch! It was better than a raw oyster. After the beach, we went out for dinner. The national meal of Korea is pronounced plue-go-wree, and the main part is thinly sliced and specially spiced beef. You sit on the floor, and they put a charcoal fire in a hole in the middle of the table. They put a

19

sort of lid over the fire and you roast the meat on the lid. You
dip the meat in hot sauce and eat it with bamboo shoots, turnip,
spinach preparations, a superhot cabbage dish (whew!), and
barley tea. The place where we ate was a huge building with
all sorts of small private dining rooms. Each room has its own
potbellied stove, and as you sit cooking your meat over the
charcoal fire, the room fills with smoke."

At Naha, Okinawa, where they arrived on November 28,
they attended morning service at the army base and found that
the chaplain was a Bible-preaching Baptist. They enjoyed a
wonderful time of fellowship with him. Naha's temperature
was eighty degrees, the humidity was 100 percent, and Lloyd
was all for giving it back to the Japanese.

A brief stop at Formosa gave time for the travelers to visit
missionaries in Taipei. En route to Subic in the Philippines,
they saw flying fish, and men in outrigger canoes. After several
storms on the way and the worst voyage in four years (according to the crew), everybody enjoyed the clear calm water and
warm temperatures on this part of the trip.

Out of Subic's population of thirty thousand, it is reported
that eight thousand are prostitutes. There was nothing to see
but bars, hotels, jeepnics (jeep taxis driven at breakneck
speeds), and girls plying their trade. The missionaries spent
most of their time at the Christian Servicemen's Center. Somewhere Lloyd had contracted food poisoning and was suffering
from pains and headache and an above-normal temperature.

By December 4, they were at the mouth of the Mekong
River waiting for clearance to go up to Saigon. The ship's crew
were now on double pay because this was a danger zone. On
the last time out three shots had been fired through the hull.
The banks, once covered with dense jungle and populated with
birds and animals, were nothing more than charred stumps
and snags as far as the eye could see.

Of the time spent in Saigon, Lloyd wrote, "The drive through
Saigon was the most dramatic yet. Such filth is indescribable.
Sewage and garbage float along the streets. Some of the peas-
ants have built houses right on the garbage dumps. The once-
beautiful city is a perpetual slum, the filth of which is incomprehensible to the western mind. Signs of war are everywhere,

with miles of barbed wire, and pillboxes and shelters on every corner.

"Here in downtown Saigon at the Christian Missionary Alliance guest house, the place has no glass in the windows. All the noise comes in: the roar of motorcycles, the beat of the band at the local tavern, the voices of people. It's super noisy. I wish they had a curfew. I can hear sirens and bombs in the distance."

When they were taken on tour by local Wycliffe missionaries, Lloyd's mind was confused by all he saw and heard. In addition, he was still suffering the after-effects of the virus or food poisoning he had picked up in the Philippines. He knew that the overland trek from Bangkok would be rough going, and he sent home an urgent appeal for prayers on his behalf. "Pray that I won't get sick. Pray that we'll get through customs without a fight. Make a big poster and put it at the front of the chapel: *All Lloyd and Louise Want for Christmas Is Your Prayers.*

At last the long sea voyage was drawing to a close. On December 8, he wrote, "Have now been at sea for one month and feel like a real sea dog. We left Saigon this morning, and by the time I woke up we were already down the river." And on December 9, "Today we landed at Sattahip, Thailand, which is a military base about one hundred miles from Bangkok. We'll be here until the eleventh. So near, yet so far!"

5

The feet of the priests that bare the ark were dipped in the brim of the water (Joshua 3:15).

On December 18, 1971, 141 days after he left home, Lloyd arrived at his final destination in Kengkok, Laos. With modern travel and transport, that seemed a long time to travel ten thousand miles! After disembarking from the freighter *Arizona* at Bangkok, Thailand, it took him a week to reach Kengkok.

On arrival at the port, the missionary party was met by Mr. Chopard and had no difficulty in getting through customs with their personal belongings. Problems arose because Lloyd, the only Canadian in the party, did not enjoy the same privileges as the Americans. He had to leave Thailand within a week by air or sea, he was informed. Then he could not go to Laos, a country without a coastline. It was almost a country without an airfield, too, but there was one at Vientiane, the capital of Laos on the border between Thailand and Laos. Vientiane was some distance from his final destination, but the only way was to fly. So off he flew. Now for the first time he was entirely alone in new and unfamiliar surroundings.

The capital proved to be no great sprawling city as he had anticipated, but a town not much larger than some on Vancouver Island. No one expected him; there was no welcoming committee, but he found accommodation of sorts in an old, abandoned and rather rickety guest house of the Alliance Mission. With his friendly outgoing manner, Lloyd soon found a friend who was both English and Christian, and with his help he began a tour of the local garages. Mr. Chopard had instructed Lloyd to try to locate a pickup truck they could purchase.

The harrowing experience of riding the streets of Vientiane

on a motorbike with his English friend was soon surpassed by the harrowing experiences of the night that followed. Worn out by the activities of the day, Lloyd settled down early in the old mission house and was soon sleeping soundly. But not for long. Soon the silent blackness of midnight was pierced by eerie shrieks and demoniacal wailing. He sat up, trying in vain to see something in the darkness. Who was it? Or what was it? Was "the howler" coming up the hall? If only his good Canadian friend, Stu, with the brawny arms were here to crush the marauders! Finally the noise died away with no apparent harm done, and he was able to sleep, only to be awakened again by the booming of artillery, or what sounded like it. Had the war come to Vientiane? The sounds seemed to come from some distance, and as there was nothing he could do about it, he shrugged and tried to sleep once again.

Next morning he found the reasons for his disturbed night. The mission house was only fifty feet away from a small Moslem mosque. The wailing and howling had come from there. And the booming of artillery was done by Buddhist priests beating on a king-sized drum. Why these performances had to take place in the dead of night was not quite clear.

Lloyd soon located a Mazda truck which he thought would serve the purposes of the mission. He paid a deposit and told the owner of the garage that the "big boss" would be there in a few days to pick up the truck. Then he booked a flight on what was called Royal Air Laos to fly to Savannakhet, some fifty-five kilometers from Kengkok, on the morning of December 18. At the *international* airport—not a whit larger than an airport had to be—he was directed to a vintage DC 3, where he crawled into the cabin with about twenty other people and eight or nine thousand mosquitoes (by his own count). He arrived at Savannakhet at nine A.M., to be met by Mr. Chopard in the Toyota. Four hours later they were in Kengkok.

Mr. Chopard had done what he could to prepare the house for the new arrivals, but it was evident that the two-year absence of himself and his wife had given "squatters" a chance to move in. They had wreaked havoc to wall screen, curtains, picture frames, pictures, food, and paper. Everything in the house was chewed by them—the rats!

23

Lloyd's personal domain was a small room, part of the Chopard's house but not actually in it. It was dark and unscreened, but he had a bed, a cupboard, a metal folding chair and a mat. It was his, and for now it was home, and after all those weeks of moving around, it was wonderful! Although supposedly the dry season, rain fell the first night he was in Kengkok, and Lloyd had to pull a blanket around him. He even needed a jacket when he got up in the morning. The missionaries had arrived, but their goods and chattels were still at Bangkok, and the truck on which Lloyd had paid a deposit was at Vientiane.

A new life was beginning for Lloyd Oppel and his companions. For years, Les and Emma Chopard had been the only missionaries of Christian Missions in Many Lands in that part of the country, and they had worked in fellowship with missionaries from Switzerland and the Overseas Missionary Fellowship. Mr. Chopard had been medic, mechanic, carpenter, technician, and farmer. Now he anticipated more time for a teaching ministry.

Writing for his missionary magazine's January 1972 issue, Chopard said, "Today a missionary must make some contribution to the society in which he finds himself before he can expect the opportunity to minister the gospel and plant local churches. . . . This is surely true in most fields and definitely so in Laos. We are pleased that those who will work in fellowship with us have something definite to offer. The ladies' qualifications are evident (Evelyn as a nurse and Beatrice as a school teacher). Lloyd has plans along social lines—building and agrarian assistance. Sam is presently in England taking an intensive, comprehensive nine month course in missionary medicine."

So Lloyd was to learn the language, help with building, and aid in putting into motion definite plans "to assist development along the line of increased food production." He was on the very edge of his Laotian experience, beginning to get his feet wet.

Language lessons and study took most of the morning hours: from seven-thirty until nine-thirty he studied with Mr. Golden

Lion, a Laotian who spoke no English; and then studied on his own until noon. The day of his second lesson was marked by the visit of two Christian friends from Dong Nang Koon who had come for medicine.

"Is this the new missionary?" they asked Mr. Chopard.

"Yes."

"Good. We want him to come and live with us today."

"But he can't speak the language yet!"

Lloyd wished that he could go with them now, live with them in the village, talk with them! But they would have to wait. Now he had an added incentive to work hard at his study.

When Lloyd had an opportunity to visit the village a short time later, he was shocked at the living conditions. Refugees were crowded into tiny huts made from bits of matting. Even the homes of the Christians who had lived in the area for some years were not much better. The plague had spoiled most of the rice crop, and the people were barely existing on meagre food. The missionaries had taken two water pumps to the village so the families could plant a rice crop during dry season.

On the first day of January, 1972, in his first letter home describing his new life in Laos, Lloyd's two great desires became evident. He wanted to find out what practical help he could give these people who were so poor and needy, so ravaged by war and suffering. And he wanted to prove to them that he had come as a friend, eager to learn their way of life and to live as one of them.

His first opportunity to be of practical help was in a clinic, repairing a lean-to on the inpatient building. He set to work remodeling what was once a kitchen, tearing off the grass matting and replacing it with wooden walls and ceiling. He put in some shelves. He soon found there was a vast difference between building in Kengkok and in Canada. In Laos, wood was at a premium, and studs were placed anywhere from two to four feet apart. Hardware was at a premium too, and Lloyd learned how to board in a wall using only three nails per board. He felt that the inexperienced local man who came to help deserved no less than a Ph.D. in nail bending (and it is hoped, later earned a similar degree in nail straightening). The same

25

man used both hands to work the saw and had to be shown that it was better to hold the board steady with one hand while sawing with the other.

Lloyd's attempts to show friendliness were boosted by the white Mazda pickup. He wrote, "Everywhere I go I wave and call to everybody. I am determined that Mr. Pooh Bow Nooat (which means 'the bearded bachelor') in the white pick-up is going to be known as the friendliest man in Laos. When I'm driving along I wave to so many people that sometimes I begin to feel like the Queen!"

6

For he shall be as a tree planted by the waters (Jeremiah 17:8).

Lloyd's program for making friends had a good beginning at the annual conference for elders held in mid-January. Christian men, carrying bundles of their personal belongings on their shoulders, came from many distant villages. Some who came from villages behind the enemy lines had not been out for three years.

Meetings at the close of each day's sessions were open to all, and the promise of a film or home movies would bring out as many as five hundred. In common with audiences everywhere in the world, when they saw themselves on the screen, they cooed and commented with self-conscious giggles. At the close of these evening meetings, Lloyd would drive the people from Dong Nang Koon back to their village because they were afraid to walk the two miles in the darkness. Following the behavior pattern of most teenage girls when a young man is behind the wheel, the girls would jump into the front seat of the truck, leaving the men, women, and children to climb into the back. The girls were soon calling Lloyd "older brother."

On the last day of the conference, he got out his handy dandy box of only slightly used eyeglasses and set up shop. Lloyd knew nothing about eye testing or prescribing glasses, but he found that the simple smile method worked very well. He would hand an elder a tract, watch him squint and falter, trying to read. Then he would offer a pair of spectacles for him to try, and then another, until suddenly a smile would break over the face of the man and he would begin to read. Unfortunately, the process was very slow because each customer

27

wanted to experiment by trying on every pair of spectacles. He sold twenty-six pair at about one hundred kip each (Lao money valued at about seventeen cents). At the price we pay for frames alone today, no wonder he won friends!

A new experience for Lloyd was a Sunday trip upriver with the Chopards to the village of Songkon, which for some time previous to this had been an insecure area. They traveled ten miles in a large dugout canoe and then some distance by foot to find 250 Lao believers gathered in a large barnlike chapel for their simple communion service. The bread was a lump of sticky rice, the staple of the Lao people. The wine was red fruit juice. The emblems and the people were a little different, and yet as Lloyd shared with them, he realized that this was true communion. Not only were they in communion with Jesus Christ, but also with Christians all over the world who came together by the same Spirit to remember the same Lord.

Lloyd found the Lao people appealing and attractive, and nothing he encountered was so frustrating as not being able to communicate with them. He was constantly amused by their concern over his single state. They were most anxious to marry him off to this girl or that, and he had to fend off their good intentions with claims that he was still too young! His heart ached as he saw suffering all around him; so many people were ill with beri-beri and tuberculosis, or so wasted with malnutrition that they resembled walking broomsticks. The inpatient house was always full to overflowing. And the people were so very poor, with so little of this world's goods! Yet they were generous in their giving and in their care for each other. They seemed to know the basic Christian concepts of love, faith, and hope in a way which North Americans did not. He felt humble before them, and he felt honored to serve where such a sweet spirit was manifested.

Nothing and no one impressed Lloyd as being so helpless as Mr. Core. Once a teacher, he had been stricken with polio and resulting paralysis, and often lapsed into a coma because of fever. When he was picked up in the truck and brought to the clinic, he was literally a bundle of bones. He could not even smile. This presented a challenge to Lloyd, who claimed he could "make friends with a boa and get a giggle from a stone." The Lao people usually appreciated his antics and went off into giggles at anything he did, but there was no response from Mr. Core, no way to reach him. Then Lloyd had an idea. Mr. Core was a teacher, right? Then he would ask him to help with language study and reading. And for the reading they would use the gospel of John!

"Oh that the Holy Spirit might open his eyes and save him as he reads the words of life to me!" Lloyd prayed.

Mr. Core read, and Mr. Core ate, and Mr. Core was tenderly cared for. At the end of a few weeks he had put on so much weight that his ribs could not be seen, and he could even walk around a little, with the aid of a stick. But he showed little interest in the words he read to Lloyd or in the message of the gospel. However, he began to take a keen interest in a private business venture of his own. In order to give him a little responsibility and to build up his morale, he had been asked to hand out numbered cards to the clinic patients so they would go in for treatment in an orderly fashion. Here was his opportunity—he could charge for early admission! For the small sum of thirty kip, he would sell a patient a low number; the others would have to be content with higher numbers and a longer wait! Those with a little extra cash and a little less time to spare would come across, and soon the kips were rolling into Mr. Core's pocket. Unfortunately for him, his business venture was not looked upon favorably by the mission, and Mr. Core's numbers racket came to a halt. Eventually Mr. Core went back to his own village, apparently well in body, but without having shown any concern about the condition of his soul.

When he had passed his first examination in the Lao language with a successful 96 percent, Lloyd began to attend the young people's meeting, one of the five gatherings every Sunday. His understanding of Lao was progressing, and he thought the Lao tones and tunes were really beautiful.

Working together with young people on the clinic building, clowning now and then to make them laugh, Lloyd was winning their affection and respect. They liked to mimic his English words, laughing over "cucumber" and cracking up when he said "do be, do be, do."

"The young people of Laos are so valuable to me, so impressionable!" he wrote to his folks. "Oh, that they might enter into the full blessedness of really knowing Jesus Christ."

Christians did not take part in the village *boons,* or celebrations in honor of the god of a certain pagoda, but they did look forward to an occasional social event. So a banquet was planned to mark the opening of the new inpatient house and to reward all those who had helped in its building. The Chopards had received a special donation from Lloyd's father in Canada toward the celebration, and this was to be the biggest feast southern Laos had seen for a long time. Christians in Kengkok and Dong Nang Koon were invited, along with the local big shots: a governor, the mayor and his two assistants, the chief of police, and the commandant—who came decked out in full regalia complete with revolver and bayonet. The Filipino staff at the USAID hospital came along, making a total altogether of 250 adults.

Missionaries and Lao helpers worked together. They cleaned up the grounds at the Chopard residence and put up parachute "tents." Tables were set up under the tents and under flowering trees. They prepared baked fish and chicken curry; they barbecued pigs; and they cooked things to go with the main dishes: sticky rice, Chinese rice (which does not stick), potatoes, and noodles. A truckload of vegetables such as mushrooms, cabbages, and onions had been brought in from Savannakhet. Iced tea and water were served with this banquet, and there was a tapioca fruit dessert. Everywhere were flowers and pretty girls. It was a "wingding to end all wingdings," and to people whose main protein supply consists of frogs and bugs, this meal was a treat indeed.

There were joyous occasions and difficult days as Lloyd became adjusted to life in Laos. He was already beginning to love the people and appreciate their simplicity and goodness. But living in a new country with a different climate, higher temperatures, and higher humidity called for some physical adjustment as well.

Apart from the attack of food poisoning on the ship and a few turns of fever, Lloyd had kept fairly well through his first four months in Laos. Then the weather became hotter and wetter, with days of one hundred degrees and lows at night around eighty. He wrote, "There are billions of gnats in the air which fly around in front of our eyes. They're attracted to warm bodies and to eyes, cuts, and sores." One day his temperature started to rise, and by the next day was 103. Two days later the fever dropped, but his hand started to swell and stiffen, a hard lump came up on his buttock, and another on one knee. "I know what I have," he said, *"Jungle rot!"*

Betty, a nurse from Wales who was working with the Chopards at the time, did not know what it was. The Filipino doctor at the US hospital said it was arthritis! But that night the pain in the abscess on his buttock prevented Lloyd from sleeping. Restlessly he paced the floor. Mrs. Chopard came to see what was the matter. She suggested he sit in hot water to try to bring the thing to a head, and at three A.M. she tried to lance the abscess. But it was still hard, and pain in his foot and hand prevented any possibility of sleep. Later they headed for the USAID hospital, where incisions were cut in hand and buttock and rubber drains stuffed in—all without anesthetic.

"This is a rough one!" Lloyd wrote home in an almost illegible scrawl. "What can I do? I can't sit. I can only use one hand. Just a little infection in an open scratch, and I've had it. All week out flat!" Even letter writing was difficult because the hand had to be kept elevated.

Removing the drains a week later was as painful as their insertion had been; one was three and one-eighth inches long! But once the drains were out, recovery was rapid.

31

7

And the daughters of the men of the city come out to draw water (Genesis 24:13).

As Lloyd visited Lao villages and saw the way the people lived and the food on which they existed, he felt there were many practical ways in which they could be helped. But first he had to experiment for himself. One of his first attempts was at keeping poultry. He soon had two Rhode Island Red roosters, some Lao hens sitting on eggs, and ten laying fowls. Lao hens could be used for setting, but they did not provide a decent meal. Mrs. Chopard brought him four fuzzy baby chicks which grew at an amazing rate when fed on laying mash. To keep the chicks warm at night, Lloyd rigged up a brooder, using a kerosene lantern. His Lao friends had never seen anything like it—neither had he, for that matter—and they wanted to know what it was. As there was no word in Lao for brooder, he had to call his contraption a "mechanical hen."

With brooding hens, he did not meet with instant success. Out of eleven eggs, three were broken, one was dead, four were not fertilized; only three hatched! From nine eggs under another hen, there were no results at all. Raising chickens was a slow and somewhat discouraging process. One of the roosters died, and the other, being of a mean and unfriendly disposition, lost his head to provide a tasty meal.

Crop raising was not very productive, either. Whether the season or the soil was to blame, Lloyd's early attempts at gardening failed.

But there was other work to be done. About Easter 1972, work began in earnest on a new inpatient dispensary which was to have a concrete floor. On the first day, Mr. Chopard

32

accidentally ran over a wooden bench, a workman cut his finger, and Lloyd dented the front fender of his truck. Not until the following day did they begin to pour concrete.

In order to get the work done properly, a Vietnamese mason was hired. This is what happened: "He figured he'd just pour the floor and level it with his handy junior-mason-size trowel. Well, what he was doing looked like the Black Hills of Bavaria, so Jack [a young American who had come to help for three months] showed him how to level it with a two-by-four board. Everybody figured this was a keen idea except the mason, who decided to sulk. What a job! All the sand and gravel had to be sifted by hand, all the concrete mixed with a hoe; all the water carried in buckets, the hundred pound bags of cement toted on our backs. We poured two-thirds of the fifteen by thirty foot floor that afternoon, Jack and I furiously troweling 'til eight P.M. trying to get a good finish. I was so pooped the next day, I flaked out for a snooze during language lesson. The next day, three teenage girls turned out to help, and we got them mixing cement, and zip, zip, zip! it was all done."

Lloyd found that he really had to hustle to keep up with those girls. He tried to list his reasons for hurrying: to prove that he was not soft; to show that proper diet kept a person going; and to show he was not too holy to rub shoulders with his fellows. He worked like a steam shovel, but the kids kept right up. Fourteen- and fifteen-year-old girls shoveled sand for eight hours. Lloyd's comment on their endeavors was, "Simply fantastic! Truly unbelievable!" One girl was "the prettiest little thing a man ever laid eyes on in her long black peasant skirt and frilly print blouse—but man, could she work!"

The two missionary girls, Evelyn Anderson and Beatrice Kosin, who up to this time had been living in Savannakhet studying the language, were now ready to move back to the Kengkok area and begin their work there. They were able to rent, at a very reasonable rate, a large house owned by Mr. Steven, a Lao Christian. But in common with most Lao houses, it had no bathroom. Lloyd installed a shower stall and then set about building a septic tank. First he dug a six-foot-deep hole in the rocky clay ground. That took sixteen hours.

Then he welded six forty-five-gallon drums end to end in sets of two. He connected the drums with four-inch pipe, then wrapped corrugated tin roofing around the barrels, poured cement in between roofing and drum. Once the cement dried, the roofing was removed. It was a pretty skookum tank! Roofing and drums were much cheaper than expensive wood, and the drums could be obtained from USAID.

This was only the beginning of working with his hands, which would include digging wells and constructing an outhouse, and finally, building a school.

8

Who . . . sendeth waters upon the fields (Job 5:10).

In 1972, the annual anxiously-awaited rains came in June—
a month late. The river through Kengkok rose and fell accord-
ingly with the rainfall. After a night of rain, it would rise as
much as thirty feet. Where it had once been possible to drive
a truck across the river the spot was now three times as wide
and thirty times as deep.

After one such night of rain, Lloyd remembered that he
had left his shoes at the bottom of the steps. Fortunately they
were under cover, so they were dry enough to wear. He slipped
one foot into a moccasin. What was that? Wet macaroni in the
toe? Oh, it was a big brown toad! He put on the other shoe.
Oh, no! Another brown toad. He shook them out and put on
his shoes. He was getting used to life in Laos; and after all,
toads in the toes would make an interesting story to write to
his little sister.

The early rains did not continue, and there were fears about
the rice crop. But toward the end of July, a downpour dropped
five inches of water one day, and the next day brought more.
Mr. Golden Lion and the other Christians were happy and
hopeful of a good crop. Now it was evident why Lao houses
were built on stilts. Tramping out to visit Grandfather (Mr.
Lion's father-in-law), who was helping him with Lao conversation, Lloyd had to wade through water to his knees.

Still the rains came, bringing fear of floods and ruining rice
plants which could stand submersion for only seven or eight
days. Lloyd did not mind walking through murky river water,
but when the path he had to take led through the mud of a
pig pen, the smell was truly revolting. He had visions of hook-

worms burrowing their way in, searching for some of the finest type O blood in Laos!

One August afternoon he paddled out with Mr. Lion and his wife to see if the rice field house was still holding together. They went through connected swamps and ponds and tiny canals in the forest—a beautiful, even romantic trip. They joked, sang, whistled as they went along. Lloyd discovered he had a hidden talent for imitating animal noises and bird calls. On the five-mile trip, they saw hundreds of acres of flooded fields. Every blade of grass, every stem of bush protruding above the water was literally covered with hundreds and thousands of ants, spiders, grasshoppers, and ticks. When they stopped for a few moments at a field house, a few thousand of them apparently decided that Lloyd would make a good refuge, and he was besieged.

At last they reached Mr. Lion's fields, or at least where his fields had been. They were covered with eight feet of water. Lloyd looked inquiringly at his friend.

"All is lost!" Mr. Lion said. "We lost the first crop through drought, now this one through flood!"

Lloyd waited for what would surely come, the wailing of distress, the complaining against God for allowing this to happen. Instead he saw only a look of firm resolve on the man's face.

"God knows about it," Mr. Lion said. "I am casting myself at His feet and depending on His mercy." He smiled at Lloyd. "This is essential for the Christian."

On their return, they found the pigpen flooded. After a struggle, they succeeded in catching the two pigs and putting them into gunny sacks for carrying to higher, dryer ground. Here a temporary pigpen had to be erected.

The waters continued to rise until there was no dry land at all in the Christian village where Lloyd was now living. Everything that had been stored under houses had to be carried up—firewood, chickens, reeds. The children had a great time catching little fish in nets. The only way to travel was by boat.

By mid-August the waters were receding. "Water—there's less of it now, only knee deep." Returning from a visit with Sam Mattix, who had now joined the missionary staff in Kengkok, Lloyd was glad for darkness and ignorance of the snakes,

36

worms, and leeches that might be lurking in the tropical waters through which he splashed. For all his wading and bathing in the waters, he came to no harm.

In that week's Sunday services, Lloyd listened to a stirring message given by Mr. Lion on the love of God and the life of the Christian, pointing out that indeed God is love, and yet it is the experience of the Christian to undergo suffering. Witness the loss of the rice crop! He gave as his authority Hebrews 12:6: "Whom the Lord loveth He chasteneth."

Later that evening the men gathered to plan a conference for some eighty new believers in eighteen villages around Kengkok, and the question of food was brought up. A young Christian offered to provide twenty-five gallons of rice stored in his granary from the previous year's crop. His entire crop for the current year had been lost in the flood. His gift was an equivalent of three weeks' salary. Lloyd shook his head in wonderment. "Next to these guys, I sure look sick," he said to himself. "I wonder who is missionary to whom? Surely *they* are teaching *me!*"

9

And they went down . . . into the water (Acts 8:38).

After months of language study, after visiting Grandfather in the Christian village to practice talking in Lao, Lloyd felt he should live with a native family to improve his spoken Lao and to deepen his appreciation of the people themselves. He called this "total immersion." He moved in with the Family of Peace—the home of Mr. Lion. His letter diary written there is signed "Lloyd the Lao."

His accommodation consisted of a two-room lean-to at the end of the house. He describes it: "The room I sleep in, about six by six feet, is too low to stand erect in, has leaf walls and a paper divider made of old cement bags to separate it from the living-cooking room. The floor is split bamboo, the roof tin. There is no refrigerator. Furniture consists of a burner to cook on, a box for food, and three thousand kip in cash (about $3.50)."

August 4 "I am trying to live as simply as possible, and didn't bring a pillow with me. I was kindly supplied with the Lao version—and for the first time readily identified with Jacob's pillow of stone. I got up at five-thirty to face my first Lao breakfast, a morning duplicate of lunch and supper. I was privileged to have a fried duck egg, which provided some consolation as I stared into my basket of cold, glutenous sticky rice—rather like petrified oatmeal. By the time I've eaten a cup of this stuff, I feel more full than if I'd consumed five pounds of steak and a kilo of french fries."

August 5 "A real storm—and life is very much controlled by the weather. Fortunately my sleeping quarters remain dry; but it was essential, once out of bed, to employ the services of an umbrella.

"Gramps was putting finishing touches to a basket, and Mother of Peace was sewing; so there we sat, squatting around a fire under the house. A scabby dog cuddled up to my feet, and smoke stung my eyes, yet there was something rich and warm despite the miserable weather, wet earth, and poor fire. Everyone seemed happy. To be pleasant and cheerful at six-thirty in the morning when everything is wet takes strength of character we North Americans know precious little about.

"When the rain let up, we launched Mr. Lion's canoe in what used to be the road and paddled over roads, rice fields, and fences to a large swamp. In this particular swamp grows a reed about seven and a half feet tall in seven feet of water, its upper leaf and sprig of seeds poking above the surface. At a certain point in the plant's development, it is possible to pull the reed free from the root. All afternoon we slowly paddled around this ten- or fifteen-acre pond and pulled reeds, one at a time. Other canoes were there, and everyone was in great spirits. The young girls teased me about my beard and frequently broke forth into little songs which became more melodious as they floated across the lilies under the sombre gray sky. Folk would pause and perhaps laugh when they saw a foreigner in a boat working with the Lao, but as soon as I displayed my great dexterity and expertise in handling a canoe, their opinion altered and I felt very much one of the gang. Everyone was so carefree, open, unsophisticated. It took four hours to fill the canoe and paddle back after one of the most enjoyable afternoons in my life—I never knew a swamp could be so beautiful. When we got back, it was time for a bath in the river, which is a sort of family swimming pool affair rather than a bath, and little naked boys jump out of trees. I was going to give the tree-jumping a try (but not in the buff) when informed that those pranks were only done by children and bathing was a serious matter!"

The family of which Lloyd had become a temporary member was that of Mr. Golden Lion. Grandfather was a former village father, and had been known as "Grandfather" for so long that his other name was almost forgotten. The same was true of Grandmother. Mr. Lion's parental name was Father of Peace and his wife was Mother of Peace. Miss Searching, a niece who lived with them, was one of the strong teenagers who helped in the building of the clinic. The oldest daughter, about twelve, was named Peace and Sorrow, and was a very shy, obedient, hard-working girl. Then came Peace and Unity, who was more outgoing and more interested in school. Nine-year-old Peace and Quiet lived up to her name. All she ever said to Lloyd was "Come and eat, sir," but she had a perpetual smile. She liked to go fishing with Grandmother. Next came Peace and Happiness, an eight-year-old boy, the happiness no doubt due to the advent of a son. The five-year-old baby of the house was a lively little spark whose name was Quest for Peace.

Lloyd found that an evening with family and friends, singing songs and telling stories, proved so much fun that he vowed never to watch TV again. When his turn came to tell a story, he cut loose with the slapstick comedy at which he excelled and which the Lao found to be the funniest kind of humor. Everybody laughed so hard they were in agony. "Man, they really howled up a storm!" he commented.

Meals at the home of the Family of Peace were hardly like home meals in Canada. Often when the call came for "grub time," it literally described what was on the menu, as the Lao people ate insects and grubs for protein. Supper might be rice, rat, whole fish, and swamp greens. Lloyd described one week's meals as progressive chicken—one chicken! Sunday morning, Mother of Peace bought a chicken. "That day we had chicken stew with nice white meat to go along with our sticky rice. Since then we have progressed—from the center of the hen out—the last meal being feet and neck stew. Oh, yummy in my tummy!"

While staying with the family, Lloyd prayed aloud in Lao for the first time. It was a long prayer—at least the pauses between each phrase were long! He began evening sing times and Bible studies with the young people of the village. Finding that no one knew the books of the Bible, he offered a chorus book as a prize to anyone memorizing them, and a Bible prize to anyone learning twenty-five verses that Lloyd selected. He felt that learning verses would be a chore for people in no way academically oriented, and he wondered if any would succeed.

When Lloyd had to leave for several weeks to help in a building project at Khum Son, he thought the whole memorizing project would die out. But when he returned and was able to spend an evening with his young friends again, he was pleasantly surprised.

"Can you say the books of the Bible yet?" he asked, turning to a young woman named Miss Grace. And she said them!

"Did anyone learn the twenty-five verses?"

The younger ones giggled with embarassment, and then Miss Light, who was sitting quietly, began to repeat the verses. She said them one by one, each with its reference, without faltering, without notes, without error. By the time she was halfway through, Lloyd was fighting to hold back the tears. Oh, it was such sweet, sweet music to him!

His time at living in a Lao home was almost over but he could say:

> Life is rich, God is gracious
> I live in a hut that isn't too spacious!

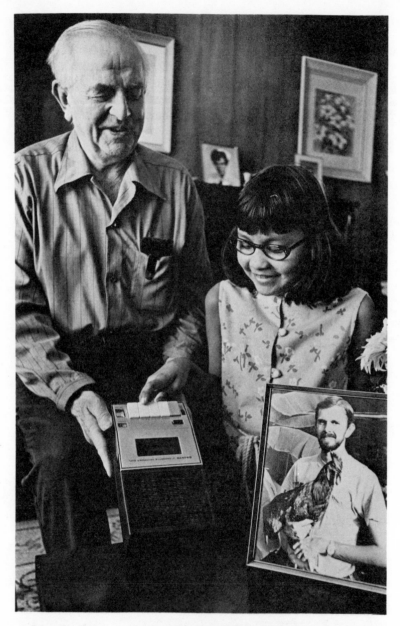

Lloyd's father and sister **Marion listen to a tape sent from** Lloyd the Lao.

10

Many waters cannot quench love (Song of Solomon 8:7).

With his tall lanky frame, dark eyes that often glowed with life and laughter, his quick wit and love of fun, and his musical ability, it was inevitable that Lloyd would arouse hopes and dreams in the hearts of some members of the opposite sex. And girls are noted for their willingness to engage in a task which most males seem to despise—that of letter writing. When mail arrived, whether it was in Courtenay, in Oakland, or in the Laotian Christian village, Lloyd was often teased because most of the letters were obviously from the feminine gender. Perhaps some even felt called to the mission field—the field of Laos?

Without a doubt, Lloyd enjoyed their letters. And he enjoyed female companionship, that of the shy, modest, hard-working Laotian girls as well as those at home. But he was heart-whole as yet. He jokingly referred to his need for a wife to cook his meals or clean his house, but he realized that for the time being, other things were of more importance. And when the time did come, he would have little patience for fluttery females who showed little evidence of the capabilities and sense of responsibility of his own sister Louise, whose example had first stirred his interest in mission work.

When it was suggested that it would be possible for a girl from back home to visit him in Laos, Lloyd warned his parents, "Remember, I'm not playing games over here, so protect me from anything that would detract from getting the job done!"

At that particular time, the job to be done was the preparations for a conference for new believers which would begin on

43

Wednesday, August 23, supper time, and would carry through until Sunday afternoon. There was a carnival camp atmosphere around the chapel, with canvas up to protect from falling rain and for outdoor food cooking. There were three sessions daily of two to three hours each, and Lloyd said they were "simply tremendous!"

Attempts by Mr. Lion and Lloyd to teach the illiterate men a chorus met with disappointment. "Even when they're singing a warming song like 'Heavenly Sunshine,' their singing makes my blood run cold!" mourned Lloyd. "They sound like thirty baying wolves!"

The study sessions were good. They liked the story of the ark—didn't they know about floods? The story of Christ casting out demons called Legion and pigs running into the sea caused great excitement, for they knew a great deal about demons, too. When asked, "What is sin?" during a teaching session, one young man said he didn't rightly know; then halfway through the teacher's explanation he suddenly interrupted with, "Man, am *I* a sinner!"

Saturday afternoon there were games: tug of war, British bulldog, dodge ball, and three deep. Hundreds of neighbors turned out to watch, and everybody had a great time. Favorite prizes were bars of soap. That evening, the place was packed out for a showing of an old 1937 silent version of *The King of Kings* with a special Lao commentary.

Lloyd wrote of that Saturday, "What a day this has been, what a new mood I'm in, why it's almost like being in love"— words he had sung in the school chorale. "After seeing the film, we Christians here all walked home together. It was really great fun to chat back and forth, carry the kids, warn each other about stepping in puddles, and share in that big happy sense of family. Man, this is love!"

Sunday, the new believers, babes in Christ, saw a large vital church in action. They saw what the church of Christ was meant to be—one in the Spirit.

Day by day, as he lived with the Family of Peace in the Christian village, Lloyd realized the closeness of the bond of love and fellowship. And as the war came closer, he came to appreciate the true peace of heart which he shared with his adopted family. One Sunday evening Mr. Chopard came to the house with news that the North Vietnamese were in a village five miles east of them, and they talked together about the protection of the Lord in any situation, realizing that their own struggle was not against North Vietnamese enemy forces, but against Satanic powers and against the evil of self which is in every man's heart. They took comfort in the apostle John's words, "Greater is he that is in you than he that is in the world," and in the knowledge that the Holy Spirit Himself was their Comforter. That night, Lloyd felt that hearts of the Lao and the missionary were truly knit together, and that this could not be attributed to the missionary's ability to overcome cultural, racial, and social differences. It could come only from the brotherhood of Christianity and the working power of the Holy Spirit in their lives making Jesus Christ the focal point of all who owned His name. They were one in Him!

11

Here will I dwell; for I have desired it (Psalm 132:14).

Soon after Sam Mattix arrived at Kengkok, he and Lloyd decided they would like to have a house of their own where they could live as a couple of bachelors. With this end in view, they bought a fairly roomy house in Dong Nang Koon, the Village in the Jungle by the Troubled Water Lagoon.

They were delighted with the property with its hundred banana clumps, twenty mango and several papaya trees, as well as bamboo, hibiscus, coconut palms, pineapples, frangipangi, and many trees and plants they had never seen before. In good shape, the place would be a real paradise, but at the time, it desperately needed a gardener.

The inside of the house was painted in psychedelic colors, hardly to their liking. So during the time Lloyd was living at the House of Peace, the young men went as often as possible to prepare and paint their new home, planning for an early October occupancy.

During this time, Lloyd's letters home were liberally sprinkled with the letters PTL, which proved to be an abbreviation for "Praise the Lord." And there was so much to praise the Lord for! After living with the Lao people, he was enjoying better health than he had since arriving in Laos. He had gained weight on the sticky rice served with squirrels' heads and rats' tails!

As they worked on painting the house, it began to take on the appearance of a very comfortable little home, PTL! One day when Mr. Chopard was in Savannakhet, he met a merchant friend who said, "That double stainless steel sink of yours has just arrived from Vientiane."

"Sink? I didn't order any sink!"

46

"That's okay, this one has your name on and is already paid for."

Mr. Chopard brought it home for the boys, and Lloyd said, "We now have the only sink in Dong Nang Koon, PTL!" It turned out that the sink had been sent by Don Scott, a friend working with World Vision.

Now the days took on an even pattern of morning study, afternoon work at the house, and evening singing, reading, and talking over the Word with Lao friends. About the middle of September, Lloyd was approached with regard to building a school in Khum Son, a refugee village about twenty-five kilometers from where he was living. Someone was needed to superintend the early stages of construction. This was the practical type of work Lloyd wanted to do, and yet after living with Mr. Lion, Father of Peace, and his family—fifty precious days he called them—it would be hard to leave and make a home in another village. There were tears on the part of the girls in the family. Miss Searching's voice, as she helped to carry out Lloyd's belongings and asked where to pack them into the truck, was rough with sorrow.

Preparation for the new venture did not take long, but possessions had to be shaken free of sundry inhabitants such as small lizards and beetles. Clothes had to be washed and debugged; needed equipment had to be packed. According to Mr. Chopard, his work would be "directing the cement work and judiciously overseeing the construction of a three-room school which World Vision and ourselves are building with an assist from USAID."

Khum Son was a poor village—unbelievably, pitifully poor. Lloyd's new home, which he shared with Number Two Carpenter, was right in the village. Pigs fought and squealed underneath, it stank, it was dirty, but was the second nicest house in the village, and he could praise the Lord for that. It was harder to praise the Lord for the work and workmen. Everything had to be done through the head man of the village, who had different ideas from those of Carpenter Number One, who had different ideas from Sam. "It's going to take a lot of grace and patience to get the work done right," Lloyd said. It also took a trip to talk things over with Mr. Chopard.

The village leader wanted a fourteen-inch pad of concrete to put the building on. "No way!" Lloyd told him. "Four inches is plenty of cement."

It was a nightmare trying to figure out where and how the building should be, but finally the layout was determined and the cement forms were in place, and actual work began.

"Wow, I really worked hard!" Lloyd said in a tape sent home. "Made some progress, but it is hard to explain what life is like out here. It's hard, tough, and rough, and yet sweet and good. I am experiencing every facet of frontier existence. And this is a spiritual frontier. Even though missionaries have been here for seventy years, there are so many brand new ears which have never heard the gospel!"

He describes how the Christians gathered together in the evening. He was invited to go along, but not to take part. They lacked confidence in his ability to speak or pray in their language. As the elders prayed over a sick friend, their dependence upon God was obvious. And Lloyd, who so liked to be independent and stand on his own two feet, realized that here in this refugee village where he was the only white man for miles, he too would learn more of his own weakness and his need for dependence upon God.

In Khum Son, for the first time he had no home, no family waiting to take him in. Talking on tape to his family in Canada, while fighting pigs grunted their static onto the tape, he praised the Lord for the homes he had known in Canada and America, with the Chopards in Laos, with the Family of Peace, and for the little things of family life which drew people close. He knew that in Khum Son, too, he would eventually find the love and fellowship he longed for. But once the construction of the school was well under way, frame up and boarded in, the roof on, and only things like doors and windows waiting to be done, he was able to return to the new home he was to share with Sam in that Village in the Jungle by the Troubled Water Lagoon.

October 14, 1972 "Guess where I am? We've finally moved into our new house! PTL."

October 22 Lloyd wrote to his sister Marion: "This was a

quiet week, a nice change from previous weeks. From now 'til Christmas I hope to do a lot of language study so my work will be easier when I'm off in different villages. In spite of bugs, dirt, and bad water, I like being in the villages with my Lao friends best of all."

He also related the story of Sam the Slop Man (Sam Mattix). "Up until recently, Sam and I have been doing our own cooking, washing, and sweeping. Not only was it a big drag, but Sam's food was enough to make you want to quit eating. And the truth is, mine was no better. Sam the Slop Man likes to experiment, so he put sticky rice, a can of imported sweet and sour, some pork, and miscellaneous grits and jowls in a pressure cooker for half an hour. It was like eating speckled wallpaper paste, but with less flavor. So when one of my Chinese friends came by and said his cousin was a cook needing work, I said, 'Have him start Friday!' "

So they had a houseboy, forty-seven years old, bilingual (Chinese and Lao), illiterate, no housekeeper, but a great cook. He had lived far to the south in a new house, with a granary full of rice. But one night the enemy came and burnt his house and granary, and he and his family fled for their lives to Kengkok.

On Friday evening, October 27, Mr. and Mrs. Chopard went to Dong Nang Koon to take the mail and to visit Sam and Lloyd in their new home. They discussed together recent political developments, the negotiations of US presidential adviser Henry Kissinger with North Vietnam. According to the news, peace was at hand, and, in fact, a proposed truce was to go into effect the next day at eleven o'clock. But they had heard the rumor machine rattle so many times, they did not take the current rattles seriously.

They also discussed their ambitious plans for the future—the building of a house for tuberculosis patients, a new chapel in the village. Lloyd outlined plans for building wells in outlying villages so he could spend more time with the local people. Sam talked of his eagerness to begin intinerating village work.

When the Chopards left, Lloyd and Sam stretched out on their beds, their minds still active with hopes and plans for fu-

49

ture work in Laos. Praise the Lord! How good He was to them! How good it was to have their own house surrounded by fruit trees.

Little did they realize that the next morning they would abandon their house in the Village in the Jungle by the Troubled Water Lagoon.

12

Behold, waters rise up out of the north, and shall be an over-flowing flood, and shall overflow the land and all that is therein;
. . . then the men shall cry, and all the inhabitants of the land
shall howl (Jeremiah 47:2).

It was 5:30 A.M. on Saturday, October 28, 1972. Sam was at the stove; Lloyd had a handful of knives and spoons and was setting the table. Suddenly there was the sound of thudding footsteps on the road below, and a young Christian from the village rushed up the front steps. Red-faced and obviously upset, he poured out his news.

"Mr. Lloyd, the Free Ones [Lao Communists] are coming from the other side of town across the rice paddies!"

"The Free Ones?"

"Yes, sir!"

"What do you think we should do? Go into Kengkok?"

The man nodded. "If there is going to be a skirmish, that would be best."

Lloyd stood for a moment, irresolute. Yes, perhaps that was the thing to do, warn the others, find out if they knew anything. Perhaps they would have to evacuate. He turned to Sam who, because of his limited knowledge of the language, had missed the import of what had been said, and explained.

"This is it! We're moving out!"

They rushed into the bedroom to collect passports and identification papers. Lloyd pulled on his slacks and shoes, and stuffed socks into his hip pocket. The farthest thing from his imagination at that moment was the possibility that he might have to wear that clothing for the next forty days.

Without pausing to close the doors, the two young men sprinted down to the Mazda truck under the house. Sam ran

51

down the driveway to open the gate. The truck was always ready to go, the tank full of gas, although up until now the prospects of an emergency had seemed remote. Lloyd took off down the driveway; Sam jumped in as the car rolled past the gate. The gate closed behind them as they left their new home in Dong Nang Koon—the Village in the Jungle by the Troubled Water Lagoon.

Two hundred yards down the lane, they turned into the main road which connected their village with Kengkok, the home of senior missionaries Mr. and Mrs. Les Chopard; and two young women, Evelyn Anderson, a nurse; and Beatrice Kosin, a teacher.

An eerie feeling came over Lloyd as he sped down the road. Something was drastically wrong! Where were the people? There was no one going to market, no one in the fields. He accelerated, roaring past a pushcart and a man trying in vain to flag down the passing car. *He probably wants to warn us that the Communists are coming,* Lloyd thought to himself. Now they began to pass armed soldiers in unfamiliar garb—green pith helmets, green uniforms—but didn't stop to find out who they were.

At the large intersection near Kengkok, Lloyd took the road to the right which would take him past the marketplace and to the Chopard home. Rounding a curve, he could see a truck parked in the street, and with it forty or fifty heavily armed troops of the North Vietnamese Regular Army.

"Yoot, yoot, yoot!"

His mind in confusion, the command didn't register, and Lloyd kept right on going. Only a few more yards and he would be past them.

What was that?

A shot! Lloyd jammed his foot down on the brakes and brought the Mazda to a stop. In that split second, the impact of what was happening hit them both.

"Lord, into Your hands we commit our lives," Sam said, aloud. Together they stepped out of the truck, hands on their heads. They were roughly escorted to a nearby fence. Lloyd was tied to a fence post, Sam to a tree. Lloyd glanced at his watch. It was 5:55 A.M.!

52

Five hours until eleven o'clock. If the proposed cease-fire went into effect at eleven, as rumored, they would soon be free. This couldn't be anything serious! While waiting, they could sing. Admittedly, their singing was not very loud for fear of provoking the soldiers, but it was sincere.

Apart from the soldiers, there was no activity on the road. When the communists had arrived, the Lao had fled. But even under communism, Buddhist monks are free to carry on their activities, and now some of them could be seen walking down the street in single file, begging for a handout of rice. But who would give them rice today? Banging on their gongs, they approached the prisoners.

"Sing to them! Sing about God's love!" Sam said.

Lloyd tried but the words would not come, and again Sam prompted as he was to prompt so often, "Come on! Don't be ashamed. Let them know about Jesus."

> *"Me kwawm nyen de nyie*
> *Me kwawm nyen de nyie*
> *Kwawm huk payay soo toum chet chi koi*
> *Hallelujah! Koi me poo soy.*

> > I am so happy,
> > I am so happy,
> > The love of Jesus floods my heart;
> > Hallelujah! I have a Saviour!"

The monks continued along the road, staring at the strange sight of two bound foreigners singing.

Lloyd watched them go. Every few minutes he glanced down the road, expecting to see soldiers bringing Evelyn, Beatrice, and the Chopards. But there was no sign of the others, no word of what had happened to them. All he could do was pray for them.

Oh, Father! It was a cry from the heart, but words refused to come. Lloyd could hear Sam's voice now and then, praying, committing the entire situation into God's hands.

As the sun climbed higher, Sam was moved into the shade where he could not be seen from the air, and was tied to a clothesline pole. A soldier brought a spade and began to dig a hole between the two young men—a hole five to six feet long and about two feet wide, with straight sides.

A grave! Was it to be a grave?

Nothing was said, but Lloyd knew that Sam was thinking the same as he. Terror tactics were common in southeast Asia, and they had heard that only three weeks earlier, communist forces had overrun a town just south of them, seizing two school teachers and gouging out their eyes, then slitting their foreheads and burying them alive.

Lloyd looked at the hole. The thought of a violent death was repugnant. Buried alive! His heart thudded against his ribs. Was that to be his fate? There was no warm glow within, he saw no roseate clouds, heard no chorus of singing angels at the prospect of martyrdom. But there was no terror, either, only a deep sense of peace. He was not afraid to die, nor was he afraid to talk to the Lord about it. "Lord, I am so young! Think how lonely my folks will be!" God filled his heart with a great calm.

He thought of the mission field of Laos, the ripened harvest, the exciting prospects. "Lord, what about the work?" Again, the calm.

Now in the valley of the shadow of death, he began to review the basic facts of his faith. "I'm a sinner, but God loves me. Mighty God, You are love!" The sense of God's nearness was overwhelming. "I stand prepared to meet God on the basis of what Jesus Christ did on Calvary."

> "My Jesus, I love Thee, I know Thou art mine;
> For Thee all the follies of sin I resign;
> My gracious Redeemer, my Saviour art Thou;
> If ever I loved Thee, my Jesus, 'tis now!"

He watched the hole deepen. If he twisted around, he could see Sam, his face turned heavenward, praising the Lord. The moments dragged by.

"Blessed assurance, Jesus is mine!" Yes, he had confidence in Christ.

Having looked at death in the face, it was almost anticlimactic when the soldier came along with an armful of wood and

54

began to make a foxhole of the "grave." So they were not to die—not just yet.

During the morning, the occupying forces were active. Some soldiers had confiscated bicycles and were riding around on them; others were allocating guns and ammunition. Reinforcements arrived. A plane circled slowly overhead. Was someone looking for the boys? They were hidden by the trees, but surely the searchers would see the Mazda truck, abandoned in the middle of the road.

At noon, Lloyd and Sam were moved and tied to the inside of a barbed wire fence, about six feet apart. For the first time they could sit on the ground and lean against a post. They were fed boiled rice and a little salt. Lloyd remembered his socks and put them on.

All morning there had been no sign of Lao people, but now along the road from Dong Nang Koon came a Christian man, Mr. Pi, riding his bicycle as if he were on his way to market without a care in the world. He ignored the soldiers as if they did not exist. Lloyd hoped he would not see the prisoners, fearing that Mr. Pi would risk his own life if he talked to them. To assure him they were all right, Sam began to sing in Lao hoping he would get the hint to stay away, but Mr. Pi kept right on coming until he stood close behind them.

"How are you?" he inquired most politely.

They did not answer, pretending they did not know him. He greeted them several times, but the boys were afraid to respond. Finally he put his hand on Lloyd's shoulder.

"God be with you, brother!" he said, and went over to Sam and did the same. Then he mounted his bike and took off in the direction of Kengkok.

Lloyd sighed with relief. He had gotten away safely! Dear Mr. Pi! Lloyd had never considered him to be much of a Christian, but how wrong he had been! How fearlessly this native believer had demonstrated true Christian love!

And half an hour later, Mr. Pi was back again, bringing with him two others from the Kengkok church, Mr. Cha and Mr. Toom. They walked up behind the prisoners sitting there in the dust and challenged their captors with a barrage of questions and information.

55

"What are you taking these men captive for?"

"Don't you know they are not enemies?"

"They're Christians! They're believers!"

"They run the Jesus Hospital!"*

"They're believers in Jesus Christ!"

"They're not soldiers. They don't carry guns!"

Again and again the three pleaded the cause of the captives, but the soldiers paid little heed to what they were saying. At last the Lao men knelt down on the opposite side of the fence and the Communists stood around, their guns trained upon them. Mr. Toom was near Lloyd.

"Oh, Mr. Lloyd, Mr. Lloyd!" he wailed. "If only we could have warned you!"

"Don't worry. God will sustain. He has promised that He will never fail nor forsake us. Don't worry about us. What happened to the others?"

His answers were confused and contradictory, and Lloyd was puzzled. It did not occur to him until much later that he was lying to protect the other missionaries.

"We must pray!" one of them suggested.

One Christian brother reached through the barbed wire fence and embraced Sam. Another put his arms around Lloyd. Together they prayed; they wept. One by one they committed one another to God's grace.

The two boys marveled at the Christian love shown to them that day by those Lao believers, and afterwards Lloyd wrote, "Jesus Christ said, 'By this shall all men know that ye are my disciples if ye have love one for another.' Right then and there, those men proved that Jesus Christ is the Son of God. They loved us, two long-nosed white boys who could hardly speak their language—foreigners!"

An officer came up and told the men to leave, but they tried to reason with him. He cocked his gun and yelled at them, "Go! go!" and at last they walked away.

Nothing else that happened that day seemed to have much significance after the Lao Christians left. During the afternoon, some of the soldiers climbed aboard the Mazda truck

*Referring to Chopard's inpatient work.

and began blowing the horn. They managed to get the motor running and floored the accelerator. They tried the windshield wipers, brakes, and headlights, but still the car didn't budge. Then suddenly, after a great deal of trial and error—with emphasis on the error—the right gear was found, the clutch popped, and 3100 pounds of Japanese steel took off at breakneck speed for a coconut palm. At the last moment the truck swerved, spewing out a passenger, and careened across the road and through a hedge, ending with the anticipated and inevitable *crunch!* Sam was laughing, and Lloyd tried to hush him, fearful that it might annoy the soldiers, but he had to admit it *was* funny. The driver staggered out of the wrecked vehicle, a bit shaken, and the momentary concern of his comrades changed to amusement.

As the afternoon wore on, the guards relaxed. The two boys were released from the fence and allowed to lie down on a low bedlike platform where the soldiers were resting. But even this measure of freedom was curtailed when a belligerent officer came along and gave orders that the prisoners were to be tied securely and guarded closely.

"You are captives!" he shouted at them. "You will go to Hanoi. Do you want to go to Hanoi?"

Even the prospect of going to Hanoi seemed preferable to execution or rotting in the wilderness.

"Yes, we will go to Hanoi," Lloyd and Sam agreed, although they knew that the choice was not theirs.

They were told to discard their shoes. "None of my comrades [literally, brothers and sisters] have these!" the soldier barked. He took away Sam's glasses, creating a real hardship to the nearsighted man.

As darkness fell, an old truck came lumbering down the road. Lloyd recognized it as belonging to one of the merchants in town, and indeed the merchant himself was behind the wheel, looking unhappy about the whole matter. The two prisoners were tied even more securely and were pushed into the back of the truck among the boxes and sacks; then they were bound to the sides of the truck. Guards sat on the wheel wells, their guns at the ready.

Slowly the old truck rolled down the road, back in the direction from which Lloyd and Sam had driven thirteen hours before. In the partial illumination of the headlights, the houses along the road appeared in an eerie glow. Soon they left behind the lane that led to their own home and Village in the Jungle by the Troubled Water Lagoon. The guards were tense, watching. The night was incredibly still, as if even the frogs and bugs feared to make a sound lest they be blasted into oblivion by the trigger-happy invaders.

Where were they going? Would they travel all the way to Hanoi in a truck? The boys asked themselves endless questions which would not, could not be answered for many long, weary days. All they knew was that they were being driven through the silent darkness into the unknown.

October 28 was over, and the black night had come. The truck left the main road and headed northeast.

13

Terrors take hold on him as waters; a tempest stealeth him away in the night (Job 27:20).

The truck with its two prisoners from Laos and their guards traveled slowly through the darkness of the October night, passing villages that seemed lifeless and deserted. But at each village, soldiers suddenly appeared from nowhere and shouted *"Yoot! Yoot!"* As soon as the truck ground to a halt, it was surrounded by soldiers demanding identification. At one stop, a soldier screamed the word for "American" and raised his rifle as if to crack Lloyd's skull, but his comrade clutched at his arm.

"We want them alive!" another shouted.

As they jogged slowly and uncomfortably over the rough roads, the young men strained their eyes in the darkness toward the direction from which they had come. They could see the sky over their beloved Kengkok light up with flares and the red dotted line of tracers arching down to earth. They could hear the successive thud of bombs. A sickness came over Lloyd. War! There was something pitiful about war, so void of mercy, compassion, and justice!

After several miles' journey, the truck stopped and the men climbed out. Aching from their cramped position, they tried to stretch. But wire bound their wrists in front and their elbows behind. The wire went from their elbows around their necks to form a noose, and then formed a leash which was held by a guard. The rocks and roughness of the road felt strange beneath their feet. Sam was barefoot, and Lloyd had only the cotton socks he had stuffed into his pocket before leaving Dong Nang Koon. They shivered in the night air.

They were led through a village and under a large building. Across an open courtyard was a typical Buddhist temple. Where were they? Under a school building? The monks' quarters? The prisoners' leashes were tied to the concrete posts which supported the building. A soldier came with a length of parachute cord in his hands.

"American rope!" he announced proudly, binding Lloyd's feet and tying them to an opposite pillar so he could not move. There was no way to lie comfortably. On his side, his arm went to sleep; he was bound too close to the pillar to lie on his back. At last he found that by lying half on his side, half on his stomach, his face pushed into the dirt, the ropes and wires did not hurt so much. A kind guard brought along a few bits of board for a pillow. Sam was tied in the same way.

They could not sleep. They could still see the lights of destruction in the west. Their cold bodies ached, their hearts ached. Sand was in everything—in their hair, their ears, their clothes. They were utterly wretched, and they were afraid of what their tomorrows might bring.

As the morning sun rose, the air began to warm. Villagers appeared and stared at the prisoners but kept their distance. An old man was told to fetch some food. He brought rice and dried frog, salt, putrified fish paste, and water.

Two officers came and began to question Lloyd and Sam.

"What is your age? Name? Occupation? Rank? Serial number? Unit?"

"We have no affiliation with the military. We are not soldiers," Lloyd explained.

"But what unit were you in?"

Lloyd tried his best, but they seemed incapable of understanding that they were missionaries with nothing to do with war or politics.

"Where were you going?" they asked.

"To market." Lloyd said, without adding that they had hoped to keep right on going when they got there.

"Do you have friends in the village?"

"No." That was true enough. Their friends were in Kengkok.

Their watches were confiscated and became the proud possession of a guard who wore both on one wrist, his sleeve rolled up to display his wealth!

Lloyd and Sam were led to the center of the village, where they were immediately surrounded by soldiers and villagers. Suddenly Lloyd was flooded with a feeling of exhilaration. This was good! This was missionary adventure! Surely God had great things ahead for them, and they would be His ambassadors in bonds. He felt ready for anything.

An officer was speaking. "You must not run, or you will be shot. Do you understand? You will go to Hanoi and be educated for two years. Then you will return to your people. But do not run, or we will shoot you!"

"No, we will not run. We will go to Hanoi!"

They were lined up single file, and the march began.

"We are going to Rome!" Lloyd called out to Sam. They were making a trip for the gospel's sake, just as the apostle Paul had done so many years ago. They were specially privileged. The prospect was exciting!

The morning's march took them along roads, with frequent dashes to take cover as planes passed overhead. Lloyd recognized one of them as the little white Porter from Savannakhet. Was it Mr. Chopard? Was he looking for them?

After hiking several miles, they came to a Lao village and were taken to the spacious veranda of the house of the village father, or mayor. The soldiers, exhausted after the offensive which had robbed them of two nights' sleep, stretched out on grass mats and were soon asleep, leaving one on guard.

Lloyd and Sam soon found themselves treated as the honored guests of their courteous host, who brought them kapok mattresses and pillows so they could rest—quite a contrast from their previous resting place! Completely ignoring the Vietnamese, he brought them food, and then a water dipper was passed.

"Have a drink."

"No, thank you." Lloyd knew the water had not been boiled.

"Oh yes!" one of the Lao piped up. "They only drink hot water." Others nodded in agreement. They knew the strange ways of foreigners.

"Do you have anything else to drink?" Sam asked.

Their host disappeared inside the house and brought out a filthy bottle. "Booze!" he said, in the Lao vernacular. "Would you like some?"

This was rice alcohol, and again the boys declined.

But Sam was thirsty. "What about a coconut?" he suggested. That would be sterile. They could drink the coconut milk.

Before long a coconut appeared, freshly cut, green. Someone had climbed a tree just to get it for them. Eagerly they watched as the man chopped off the end. Already they could taste that delightful drink! And then they watched, aghast, as the man carefully poured the milk from the coconut into a black tin kettle, and from that into a dirty red plastic cup. Alas for their hopes of an uncontaminated drink! But they dared not express their feelings—they must show their appreciation and drink what was offered. That night's supper was rice and dog stew which—after his indoctrination into Lao menus, Lloyd was able to enjoy until the sight of intestines and a few other choice morsels took the edge from his appetite.

When Lloyd and Sam began to sing a few songs, the interest of villagers was aroused, and about twenty Lao men gathered on the porch. The North Vietnamese Army did not interfere, and Lloyd was able to talk to the men and the village father. It was soon discovered that they had mutual friends in Kengkok.

"When you go to Kengkok, tell them you saw the one with the beard," Lloyd said, and the father agreed. This was how the first rumor of the boys' whereabouts and the story of the coconut (slightly twisted as rumors are apt to be) first reached friends on the outside.

After supper they set out again, and as darkness fell, they approached a large village. Judging from the noise, a festival was in progress, and the North Vietnamese, fearful that some Royal Laotian troops might be there, forced their captives to hide in a thicket. Lloyd entertained himself by tearing leaves into patterns of a fish and a cross, and by talking to one of the guards, a young fellow about his own age.

"We will not stop fighting until we kill all the enemy in Vietnam, Laos, Cambodia, and Thailand!" he asserted.

They marched on in total darkness, the trail lit only by the faint stars high above. Lloyd could see, but the guard who held his leash tripped continually. Each time he tripped, he pulled on the wire leash and on the wire looped around Lloyd's neck, nearly ripping his head off. The only thing he could do was grasp the loop with his hands and absorb the jerk. Lloyd was tiring. His socks were completely worn through, and the trail hurt his feet. Sam, with no protection at all, complained that ants bit his feet and ankles. Late in the night, the guards took them from the main trail to a narrow path through a thicket of bushes. The path led to a North Vietnamese Army camp with bunkers and dugouts everywhere, and hammocks strung between small trees.

Utterly exhausted, Lloyd flaked out on the jungle floor, too weary to care about ants or other insects. They were given plastic sheets, and once again their feet were bound, and the boys were tied up as they had been the previous night. They slept.

Suddenly Lloyd awakened. What had happened? His hands burned like fire! The pain was excruciating, the wire biting into his flesh. Somebody had to do something!

"Guard! Guard! My hands—oh, my hands! Undo them! Take the wire off my hands!" He was beside himself.

The guard came over and fingered the wire, letting loose with a mean little chuckle. He did nothing to release the pressure that was sending the searing pain up Lloyd's arms.

"You don't even want to help me!" Lloyd whimpered.

The guard laughed. As Lloyd looked up at that grinning face, something snapped inside. Hate boiled up deep within. *Buddy, if I didn't have these wires on me, I'd get up and smack you in the kisser! I'd—I'd kill you!* He did not say the words aloud; he did not dare show what he felt.

As the guard walked away, Lloyd's fierce anger cooled a little. He was in their power, and they hated him. What could he do? Oh, he knew the words Christ had said, "Love your enemies . . . do good to them that hate you." How could he love these people who had no vestige of pity, who could take a sadistic delight in his suffering?

He tried talking to Sam, hoping for sympathy, but that did not help much.

"Listen, we're prisoners!" Sam said. "In their eyes we deserve to be hurt, don't you understand?"

And Sam went on to talk about all the things they had to be thankful for—the fact that they had plastic over them, that they were a little warmer than the night before. They could be thankful the night would not last forever. They could be thankful—

Lloyd turned away restlessly. He was in no mood to listen to sermons on thankfulness now. He almost hated Sam at that moment—the sanctimonious twerp! Why wouldn't he get with the program? Thankful? Nuts!

But as the darkness began to lift, the Holy Spirit came to minister, to cool the fevered spirit, to pour a little cold water on the inferno of hatred, to gently suggest that this was *His* program and shouldn't he—Lloyd—get with it? He could, and eventually he did, but it was a long process.

The new day brought renewed vigor and determination to live. Lloyd realized it was foolish to nurse bitterness, and he tried to put the night's happenings from his mind. A guard came to untie their feet and loosen their hands so they could eat. Soldiers gathered around and began their string of questions—questions they were to be asked wherever they went: How old are you? Are you married? Do you have a girlfriend? Are your parents alive? How old are they? Do you have brothers and sisters? On and on they went, like a stuck record repeating the same phrases over and over.

From vines which grew in the thicket, Lloyd fashioned the framework of a hat. He shoved leaves through the opening to keep out the fierce rays of the sun. He felt good that morning, striding along the trail, ready to face the challenge of a rugged situation, and he sensed that Sam felt the same way. With God, all things were possible! They just had to keep on walking.

Late that afternoon they stopped under a few trees in a quiet, peaceful setting of rolling hills. The boys had had little time for personal devotions, but now they could have a prayer meeting and remember their fellow workers in Kengkok. They knew how keenly Mr. Chopard felt his responsibility, how concerned he would be over them. They knew that when the news of their capture reached home, their parents would need an extra portion of comfort and the peace that passes understanding. Looking up at the serene expanse of the blue sky above them, Lloyd experienced the same peace.

"Peace like a river is flooding my soul!" He loved that song, and right now he knew something of what it meant. When he tried to express something of his thoughts to Sam, he saw that Sam's face was set and troubled.

"What's the matter, man? You were the one telling me to be thankful!"

"It's getting to me. I'm afraid. Afraid of what they are going to do to us here on the trail. They could kill us, get rid of us right here, and nobody would ever know what happened to us."

"If that is what they are planning, why are they keeping us alive?"

Sam shook his head. "I don't know. I'm just scared."

Time and again they were to struggle with the Christian's fiercest predator—fear. They would walk in the dark cloud of uncertainty, never knowing what a day would bring, but they would learn that they were not alone and that God's promises never failed.

When darkness fell, they took off at double pace, which created added misery for Sam, who could hardly see at all and had to be led by guards. There was some talk of riding in a truck, and hopes soared at the prospect of a ride to Hanoi. As they walked through a village thick with North Vietnamese soldiers, Lloyd thought he could hear the voice of someone reading aloud. The voice came from a little house, and he walked over to it and peered in through a crack. An old man was sitting crosslegged before a smoky little lantern, and he was reading from a large red book. Lloyd listened. Those words were sweetly familiar. The man was reading the Bible. There in the midst of militant Communism was the eternal Word of God!

On the other side of the village, the prisoners were crammed into the back of an army truck and roared off into the night. As soon as his eyes became adjusted to the darkness, Lloyd realized they were traveling through a bombed-out area. He could see the branches of the trees, torn and stripped of leaves. The terror of war gripped him again. The soldiers, too, seemed nervous, watching the sky. Would they be bombed? Surely no one would spot the truck, but the motor—why must it make such a noise?

The ride was a short one. Once they had forded a river, they climbed out of the truck and walked again. The darkness was so deep it was impossible to see the path, and Sam stumbled painfully again and again until the guard got the idea of warning him of hazards. At another village, a house was commandeered, and its sleepy owner was sent staggering off into the night to find a sympathetic friend who would take him in. Lloyd and Sam were tied down to the floor, but this time they had kapok mattresses between them and the boards, and they could praise the Lord for that! They forgot the ropes and fell into deep sleep.

It felt good the next morning to lie perfectly still on those mattresses while the rays of morning sun filtered through chinks in the eastern wall. Lloyd saw that Sam was on the move. He had found a use for the kapok which was escaping from a hole in the mattress. He had been given a pair of socks, and now he was stuffing them with a cushion sole to make shoes. After that, he spun bits of string and used the string to draw diagrams of a palm tree, a water buffalo, a pig. The soldiers watched with interest. When Sam made a hill with a cross on it, one soldier remarked he knew what that was about.

The new shoes proved quite successful on the trail.

"Aha! What exceptional footwear I am wearing today. I must patent this idea when I get home!"

Lloyd was amused at Sam's happiness. The shoes may be as comfortable as Hush Puppies, but they lacked something in appearance. Sam appeared to be suffering from elephantiasis! Now the important thing was to keep the shoes dry by stepping over puddles and jumping over streams.

At last they were faced with the inevitable—a river. How would Sam get across without getting the precious kapok shoes wet? While they were wondering, the soldier with Sam's leash handed it back to him, took off his own pack, and rolled up his trousers. Then he told Sam to get on his back. And

66

there was Sam—all six feet of him, draped over a man nearly a foot shorter than he, and certainly much lighter. The same carrying courtesy was extended to Lloyd. The whole thing was incomprehensible to the prisoners. They were bigger and heavier than their guards, yet they were being carried. For the rest of that day and part of the next, they were taken across every stream until Sam's conscience began to trouble him, and after all, his feet *were* wet.

Sam's feet had large blood blisters on the soles, and walking was becoming increasingly difficult for him. Somewhere, somehow, shoes would have to be found.

Evening brought them to some houses on the edge of ripe rice fields. An assortment of chickens clucked under one house, and an old granny could be seen preparing food over an open wood fire. This was rural Laos indeed! They were taken into the house and settled in one corner, and Lloyd lay back for a presupper nap.

"Lloyd, don't you think we should tell these people about the Lord?" Sam said.

Lloyd nodded. The spirit was willing, but the flesh was very weary. It would be so much easier to sleep, but he began to sing and talk to the people.

"Do you know who Jesus is?"

"No, we don't!" they replied.

"Jesus is the Son of God. God is the one who made everything. You know about the spirits?"

"Oh, yes!" They all revered the spirits.

"Well, Jesus is greater than all the spirits!" Lloyd assured them, and went on to explain the gospel message as well as he could in the Lao language.

As they talked to the people, the boys noticed an ancient book hanging on the wall above the place where they were to sleep, and they asked if they could look at it. No one knew how to read it, but the book apparently contained mystical writings of Buddha. They leafed through it carefully. On the wall above the place where the book hung was a little shelf with offerings to the spirits.

Lloyd remembered that it was October 31—Halloween—a night on which the devil makes fools of saints and sinners alike as they glibly mimic the powers of evil. But in that lonely Lao house, there was no frivolity or amusement associated with the sinister spirits which captivated their very souls.

That night the two young missionaries lay in the dark, their heads resting under the spirit shelf. They were in the heart of Satan's domain, and yet they slept untroubled knowing that "greater is He that is in you, than He that is in the world" (1 John 4:4).

14

He leadeth me beside the still waters (Psalm 23:2).

NOVEMBER 3-8

On the seventh day of captivity, Lloyd and Sam saw their first full-fledged, well-established North Vietnamese outpost camp in Laos. At this time they were escorted by five soldiers, headed by the one they named "Sarge," who was still wearing their watches on his arm. The camp was a series of "hooches," or shacks made of bamboo, thatch, and plastic sheeting.

The boys were taken to one of these hooches and told to stay on a sizeable platform bed at one end. The hooch had a table where the guards sat playing their endless card games, enthusiastically slamming down cards until their shouts and laughter drowned the sounds of the jungle. In addition to playing cards, they smoked opium pipes to pass the time. The pipes were made from a section of bamboo with a small bowl to hold the tobacco at one end. The smoker would suck furiously on the other end until the smoke was drawn through the water. He would fill his lungs and then lean back and allow a cloud to float from his mouth. He only took one snort at a time, sufficient to solve the immediate problem. Lloyd noticed that if more than one snort were taken, the smoker showed signs of tripping, that is, giddiness, dilation of pupils, and change in coloring of the eyes. The ritual of smoking and ceremoniously passing around the pipe took a good deal of time. The guards informed them that every soldier smokes the water pipe.

Confinement to camp brought idle hours, and the two prisoners sang to pass the time. The light frothy songs of happier circumstances held little appeal, but they enjoyed the hymns of depth and meaning. There was time for meditation and thought sharing.

"I was lying deep in thought and meditating on God's faithfulness," Sam told Lloyd one day. "The unknown future was eating away at me, and I realized the only constant amid it all was the constancy of God's care. I was so overcome by the love of the eternal Father that I wept. I realized I was a complete pauper, a prisoner, and there was no hope for me apart from God, yet I could say

> Great is Thy faithfulness, O God my Father,
> There is no shadow of turning with Thee.
> Thou changest not, Thy compassions they fail not;
> As Thou hast been Thou forever wilt be."

Their first Sunday on the trail had been a nightmare, and they had given little thought to the day. But on this, their second Sunday, they were not on the move. From their morning meal, they saved a lump of rice and a little water for their remembrance feast. Perhaps the emblems were a little different from those Christ used on the Passover night, but His Spirit was in their midst as they remembered Him.

That day they were allowed to sit outside in the sunlight and were given knives and bamboo from which they were able to fashion their own chopsticks. Lloyd held up his knife, grinning.

"They must trust us, to let us have knives," he said.

"Yes, and did you see what they did this morning? When the soldiers went outside they left their automatic rifles within a few feet of us. I guess it is up to us to prove trustworthy!" Sam said.

Lloyd nodded, and his eyes sparkled. "You know what I was tempted to do? Carry out their weapons and hand them to the soldiers, and say 'Hey, you forgot these!' "

That Sunday brought the luxury of a bath with running water. They were taken to a shallow, clear, fast-flowing river and given soap to wash themselves and their clothing. Even as they splashed about in what seemed to them a veritable tropical paradise, their thoughts turned to home and the family and friends who were no doubt desperately concerned about their welfare.

Even in a camp with moderately agreeable surroundings, inactivity was boring. Monday brought no hope of moving onward to Hanoi. Were they to stay indefinitely here in a jungle camp, forgotten, to rot away of disease? It was good to have time for meditation, but Lloyd found that too much time led to self-pity. Here he was, young, vital—but a captive. He was restrained, not permitted to pursue any activity. And suddenly he remembered a lady in his own home town. She was married, had children, lived in a free society, had her own ambitions and aspirations, yet she too was held in a bondage from which death or the rapture could be the only release—the bondage of a wheelchair. How could he pity himself when he thought of her captivity? He needed to get his eyes off himself and look to Jesus.

" 'Jesus, keep me near the cross . . . in the cross, in the cross, be my glory ever.' Please Father, keep me near the cross," was his prayer.

One day the soldiers went hunting. Lloyd wondered what they hoped to find; he had never seen anything larger than a squirrel during his stay in Laos. All they got that day was a bird which they had wounded in the wing. They put it down on the table, and it stayed there motionless, its long slender beak forming a graceful arc in the candlelight.

Perhaps he could have a friend or a mascot, Lloyd thought, and bent to examine the little creature more closely. He noticed that a thread had been pulled through each eyelid and tied across the top of the head, sewing the bird's eyes shut. How could they? The poor thing!

"You've sewn its eyes shut!" he accused. "What did you do that for?"

"Well, when it is blind, it cannot see; and when it cannot see, it does not know the danger; and when it does not know the danger, it does not want to escape!" a soldier explained.

As Lloyd stared at the soldier, a Bible verse flashed through his mind: "The god of this world hath blinded the minds of them which believe not, lest the light of the glorious gospel . . . should shine unto them" (2 Corinthians 4:4).

Four days in camp. Were they ever to get on their way again? About noon of the fourth day, some officers came in, and Lloyd and Sam expressed to them their desire to go to Hanoi.

"Two days walking, one day in a truck, and you will be there!" one of the men assured them.

Their hopes soared. They had heard the rumble of trucks in the distance. Surely they would soon be on their way to Hanoi.

15

Giving thanks for all things (Ephesians 5:20).

It was good to break camp and get underway again, especially if it meant they would reach Hanoi in two or three days. Perhaps the peace agreement had already been signed and they would soon be free! But the jungle which kept news of them from the outside world, also kept news of the outside world from them. They could not know that the peace talks were dragging on and on, nor that the days on the Ho Chi Minh trail were to drag on and on for them.

Now and then they passed through small Lao villages. In one, the women were just returning from the fields, carrying bunches of long green beans. Apparently some of them had never seen white men, and they came to stare at Lloyd and Sam. An old granny was awestruck at the size of Sam.

"My goodness, what an enormous person!" she exclaimed, adding superlatives that matched him up to Paul Bunyan.

The character of the country changed, and they began to pass through more dense jungle. Lloyd noticed a couple of leeches clinging to his ankle. What could he do? Weren't you supposed to burn them off and cauterize the wound? They came off without difficulty, but the resulting wound took a long time to heal, and the flesh around it felt like jelly. In the thick of the jungle they came to a North Vietnamese Army garage and service center, and immediately the mechanics gathered around to look at the prisoners. Some of the mechanics were hostile, others merely curious. Lloyd and Sam sang for them and tried to answer their questions and explain who they were. But the North Vietnamese failed to grasp that one was

Canadian and the other American. What was the difference, they asked, peering at the two rough-looking characters in front of them. Oh, they had it! Americans were blue-eyed and Canadians brown-eyed.

The friendly conversation did effect some change in the attitude of the mechanics, a change which proved beneficial. For ten days, the boys had traveled practically barefoot, and in that time they covered about a hundred miles. All they had for their feet were socks and pieces of cloth bound together with bits of vine, and these would be of no use in rough mountainous terrain. The mountains were just ahead. But the Lord knew the mountains were there! Hadn't He made them?

When the mechanics saw the condition of Sam's feet, they were obviously concerned and brought along some canvas rubber-soled shoes for the boys to try on. Like Cinderella's stepsisters, Lloyd tried to squeeze his feet into a pair, but they were too short. That problem was remedied with a machete—used on the shoes, not on Lloyd's toes! The toeless shoes fit fairly well and proved most serviceable. But with Sam, there was no simple solution. By Vietnamese standards, his feet were enormous, and nothing would fit. The mechanics proved once again the old adage, "Where there's a will there's a way," and made large rubber soles from truck tires and cut straps from an inner tube to fashion rubber-tire sandals! Had it not been for the shoes provided that day, Lloyd's and Sam's feet would have been mutilated on the rough trail. Once again they had something for which they could praise the Lord!

That night they were both tied down to a makeshift single bed—not very spacious for a couple of six-footers—and were given only one blanket. Whoever had the blanket was temporarily warm, and the other had to keep close enough to share the generated warmth. *A good thing we're friends,* Lloyd thought to himself as he tugged at the blanket. Would they still be, come morning?

The next morning they were on the trail again. Sam was soon having foot trouble again, as blisters began to form under the rubber straps. They were surprised to see much more activity on the way, and now women in great numbers—wearing their typical white blouses and black trousers—were riding in

74

the trucks with the men. When they reached a command post at the intersection of several truck roads, they were taken to the central area and once again were immediately surrounded by a crowd of curious soldiers. Sometimes the circle of hostile faces seemed more frightening than bare prison walls could ever be, and today they were afraid. But they tried to be friendly, to smile, and to answer questions put to them. Apparently their efforts paid off, as a soldier brought them two cereal bars made in China. The boys noticed that the contents were listed on the packets in English, giving the nutritional value of the bars. They provided a welcome change after two weeks of an improperly balanced diet.

Although the post was on the truck road, any hopes of going on by truck were soon disappointed, and Lloyd and Sam were taken up the hill to spend the night in a small hooch which had served as an infirmary. Their guard that night was young and cocky, belt low on his hips, hair slicked back. "Punk!" Lloyd thought to himself.

"What were you doing in Laos with the Americans?" the guard asked Lloyd. "You are a Canadian, aren't you? What were you doing with a pistol? I found one in your house."

"No way!" Lloyd said. "I don't even have one. There was never a pistol in my house."

"Oh yes, there was. You know what else I found?" His eyes took on an evil gleam. "Letters from your fiancée!"

"I don't have a fiancée, so you couldn't have found letters."

"But I did!" he insisted. "Want to see them?"

"Yes, show them to me!"

"No. You want to know something else? You're lucky to be alive. Those truck drivers out there wanted to kill you." He stuck out his chest and swaggered a bit. "I spoke up for you and stopped them."

The guard's consideration for them was shown that night when they were tied down tighter than usual. But at least they had a blanket each!

The next day was November 11, Armistice Day, but Lloyd and Sam were too involved in the current war to remember those of former years. Hiking was becoming more difficult because of the uneven terrain and frequent hills. The growth was heavily tropical, and they saw plants with leaves five feet long and four feet wide. The soldiers said they were edible. There were date palms and enormous trees interwoven with huge vines, the stems of which were eight inches in diameter.

The night's stopover was in a large camp under trees by a fast-flowing river. Pigs and chickens were rooting about. During the day they had passed North Vietnamese teenage girls at work digging foxholes. In the camp there were more girls.

"Are we in North Vietnam?" Sam asked.

"No. You won't be there for a couple of weeks yet!"

The curious crowd gathered as always and began shooting the familiar questions at them. Not a friendly face was to be seen. No one responded to their feeble smiles.

"Do you love America?" they asked Sam, and he was afraid. What could he say?

"Yes, I love America because my family lives there and it is my home."

It was a relief when the guards returned and told them to move along. Sam's leash was dragging behind him, and he picked it up and handed it solemnly to his guard. His action brought a round of laughter from the crowd.

The next morning Sarge came to say goodbye. There was to be a changing of the guards at this point. They wished each other good luck.

"Thank you, thank you!" They all said over and over, and then they all laughed. Those words had become a joke on their journey. Lloyd and Sam had learned the value of being thankful and of expressing their thanks to others. Whenever their captors did something for them, they said thank you in Lao. The guards had never heard this before and thought it very strange that the prisoners should thank them at all. After a while, they themselves would say, "Thank you, thank you," before the boys could get the words out. Now, as the guards disappeared down the trail, they were calling out, "Oh, thank you, thank you!"

Travel resumed under the watchful eyes of three guards. There was an officer they nicknamed "Pops" because he had the letter *P* on his belt buckle, and because he lived up to the name; another guard who was short and happy-go-lucky they called "Rabbit" because of his size and demeanor; and the third was so uncommunicative, he earned no name at all. They continued to pass groups of soldiers on the way, and parties of junior-age children were traveling south under the supervision of adult leaders. Sometimes the soldiers stopped to enquire about Sam's feet, which were obviously hurting. Pops did his best to procure shoes for Sam, and at one camp he succeeded in locating a pair. Sam managed to squeeze one foot into a shoe. With the toe cut out, he could wear it. But the other shoe was for the same foot!

The boys spent one night in a little lean-to right in the middle of a camp. Sam fell asleep almost at once, but Lloyd experienced difficulty in dropping off. When the officers saw that he was awake, they hurled abuses at him. Another night the two were put into a storage hut and then lowered through a trap door to a bunker below. Space was limited, the air foul, and the place infested with rats.

On the trail, Rabbit always took the lead. When he came to a difficult section, he would hop, skip, and jump in a typically rabbit-like way. But Sam could not see well enough to follow, and the rough trail was a constant hazard. Always, his feet hurt. That day he developed a terrible thirst, drinking three times as much as Lloyd. It was hard going for both, and they wondered how long they could keep it up. That night, when they climbed wearily into their hooch, Lloyd felt such a wave of depression creeping over him that he could not push it away. When it came to their prayer time, he shook his head.

"You first, Sam!"

Sam began with his usual list of thank-yous. Lloyd drew in his breath sharply. No, not that again! What could there be to thank God for tonight?

"Lord, thank You for the flower I saw today. I couldn't quite make it out because my eyes aren't in focus, but it was small and blue and reminded me of the forget-me-not. Father, You never forget us, for You have said 'I will never leave thee nor forsake thee, so that we might boldly say, the Lord is my helper and I will not fear what man may do unto me.' "

Sam went on praying, but Lloyd could not hear what he was saying. Tears filled his eyes and coursed slowly down his cheeks. "I will not fear. I will not fear—because You will not leave nor forsake me. Lord, You are here with me in this filthy hooch. I know it; I believe it. I will not fear!"

In some respects, Pops seemed to be an angel from God. Lloyd was sure he was God-sent, if not actually an angelic being. That night they lay in darkness, uncomfortable, alone, and fearful. They could hear pigs rooting below. Someone climbed the ladder to that abandoned Lao hut and joined them in the darkness. It was Pops! First he talked to Sam, then came over to Lloyd.

"Are you lonely?"

"No." Lloyd was unwilling to admit that he was.

"Missing your wife?"

"I'm not married."

"Missing your parents?"

"No, not really. I am okay."

Pop sat beside him, patting him on the shoulder, pulling the blanket around him. He was so fatherly, so kind and loving. Lloyd fought to keep back the tears, but it was no use. He was glad for the darkness.

It was Pops, too, who eventually came up with a pair of canvas shoes which—once the toes were removed—would fit Sam, and which served him for the remainder of their time on the trail.

The strain of captivity, the forced marching, and the poor food began to take their toll. For a few days Sam was ill and found it difficult to eat. The weather turned colder, and they were grateful for two long-sleeved shirts which were given to them. They were still passing soldiers going south, and they experienced what Lloyd called "walking the gauntlet." Sam was first in line and apparently took the soldiers by surprise, for they did no more than holler and scream. By the time they reached Lloyd, a few yards behind, they were primed for action. They swung out at him, hitting him on the backs of the legs, the head, or the seat. It did not really hurt him physically, but he found it hard to be treated with disdain in that way. After all, he was not their enemy!

The trail now took them over mountains in which great flights of steps had been cut. There might be two, three, or even four hundred steps to climb, and then down the other side. The going was extremely rugged, and they put all their waning strength into the business of forcing legs and feet to obey their will as they plodded up and down. Afterwards, they could hardly remember what had happened on those days.

They remembered walking through long grass to a river where their guards signaled to a man in a long Vietnamese boat to come and carry them across. Hundreds of soldiers on the bank screamed and waved as they passed, but they landed downstream and were soon hidden again in the grass.

16

Thou shalt forget thy misery, and remember it as waters that pass away (Job 11:16).

The trip to Hanoi, which at one time was to take two days' walking and a day in a truck, was lengthening out. It was three weeks since Lloyd and Sam had been captured, and their way still led through the "wilderness." There was monotony in each day's pattern of hiking, stopping to be stared at, sleeping in a shack or a bunker. It was inevitable that some things would be forgotten and others stamped indelibly on their minds, but Sam has a photographic memory, and the "photographs" of what happened on the Ho Chi Minh trail are imprinted on his memory in an orderly manner. He recalls what happened when Lloyd had his first serious bout with malaria.

Early in the afternoon of November 18, they reached a camp in a clearing beside a stream. At this time they were in the care of a man they called "Prof" because of his interest in studying English. Prof led them through the camp and past the curious crowd to a long cabin in a secluded area. That day Lloyd had traveled with a great show of energy, almost impatient with Sam, who was not feeling well and found it hard to keep up. But Lloyd's brief burst of energy had been stoked by a mounting fever; that evening his head was spinning, and his long frame shook with chills. Prof was concerned and went for a medic. Lloyd's temperature was 104.

That night and most of the next day, Lloyd slept restlessly, tossing from side to side. He became delirious, and the medic came with vials of antibiotics and a pot of steaming water with sterilized instruments. Lloyd was given an injection.

As he watched Lloyd lying there so desperately ill, Sam faced another fear—not the fear of hostile people, but the fear of loneliness. He records, "I was very concerned for Lloyd's life—afraid that he might die out there in the middle of the jungle and leave me alone. I really pled with God." His prayers were answered, and Lloyd began to show some improvement.

These were days of inactivity for Sam. He sang songs until he had sung all he could remember, and he still had a lot of time left over. He was expected to provide English lessons for Prof, but he experienced great difficulty in understanding anything the Prof tried to pronounce in English, and not much progress was made.

Both boys were suffering from almost continual diarrhea and from lack of nourishment. Lloyd was unable to swallow anything more than a little rice. But somewhere, Prof found a can of powdered milk and a plastic bag of sugar cubes and brought them with their hot drinking water. They were able to mix up a drink of hot sweet milk, which tasted great and was nutritious as well. That welcome supply of milk and sugar lasted for several days.

The event which marks November 20 in Sam's memory was, "My ropes were completely removed."

Lloyd was a little stronger the next day, but he still had too much fever to travel. They were able to go down to the stream, where they tried to wash themselves and their clothes, but the weather was so cold and wet that drying the clothes presented a problem.

Prof insisted that they make an attempt to travel the next day, promising an easy walk to a destination only forty minutes away. The trail was a steep climb on slick mud and up steps, and every sliding stumbling step took its toll.

"How long since our last rest? Is it ten minutes yet?" Lloyd asked Sam time and again.

"No, only three or four!"

"But I can't go—any—further."

"Come on, man!" Sam urged. "We have to keep going!"

"I keep blacking out—I don't even know where the trail is!"

"I know you feel that way. It was rough going for me a few days back, too!"

"My head is pounding!"

Their progress was slow through the thick wet jungle, over the hill and down the other side. They crossed a rickety bridge of bamboo and pole construction, to climb again to a small camp still under construction—their destination for that day.

The camp was in the charge of a Vietnamese officer, whom they immediately and privately named "Tough Guy" because of his attitude and his repeated threatenings to kill them if they made any false moves. Lloyd and Sam were housed in a temporary structure of bamboo frame covered with green plastic. Beds were made of split bamboo; the floor was dirt. Ends of their shelter were open, and a cold wind blew through. While Lloyd stretched out to rest, Sam went down to the kitchen and returned a short time later with "one of the best meals of the trip in Laos": rice and scrambled eggs with chopped green onions and pork fat. Tough Guy even allowed them extra blankets that night, and they slept well.

17

There was no water but mire (Jeremiah 38:6).

NOVEMBER 23-25

On November 23, Lloyd and Sam were given a good breakfast plus vitamin pills, and they soon set out again on the trail. After a wet night, the clay ground was slick and wet and pulled at their shoes. Lloyd felt stronger and was able to keep up with the others, but his thirst was insatiable. The country they were traveling through was changing. They saw bare rock outcroppings and protrusions with clumps of ferns and foliage. Great trees were intertwined with leafy vines which dripped water on their heads. Now and then, houses of tribal people could be seen.

Using both their hands and feet, they clambered carefully along the wet rock, breathing little prayers that they would not slip and fall. Off the main trail, they followed an overgrown path down a steep hill. Sam slipped and traveled some distance on his seat. The path brought them to a fast-flowing river with a single log bridge and a handrail made of vine, moored at both ends, but very wobbly. They longed to rest and wash in the river, but they were allowed to stop only long enough to clean off the leeches. Prof was tiring as much as the boys with the travel, and all were relieved when rest stops were permitted.

They came at last to the large camp where they were to spend the night. A guard with a red star on his helmet led the prisoners to the river to wash their feet, then brought them back to a small enclosure. Immediately the foreign prisoners became the current attraction for camp people, especially the children.

When their meal of rice and pork was brought, Sam said, "Lloyd, do you know what day this is in America? Thanksgiving!"

"Then *you* pray."

Sam gave thanks for the food, and then he added, "Father, we pray that our folks may know our condition and whereabouts, and that they will enjoy their Thanksgiving dinner. Don't let concern for us keep them from enjoying this day."

They strung hammocks under the trees and rigged up tents of plastic sheets to keep out the rain. They retired early that night, snug and fairly comfortable, with the realization that they too could thank the Lord for His goodness.

The rain that lulled them to sleep during the night mired the trail and made the going difficult. Water had filled the prints of countless feet until the trail looked like a barnyard. The hikers found it hard to keep their shoes on, and yet they were needed because of the sharp rock protrusions. At one stream crossing, the going was so treacherous they went from rock to rock on all fours. Perhaps because of his poor vision, Sam fell several times that morning, but he happened to land on soft, wet grass and didn't hurt himself.

"Do you know what verse keeps coming to my mind?" he asked Lloyd. " 'Now unto him who is able to keep you from falling.' But maybe I'm taking it too literally!"

They traveled miles through bush and jungle, along trails so overgrown they were difficult to follow. Sometimes they climbed little ladders over huge logs, or walked along logs, or ducked under them. All the way the trail was muddy.

Near some North Vietnamese vegetable fields, the boys were offered fruit which resembled grapefruit but turned out to have super thick skin and a super sour taste. They tried to eat it, not wishing to offend the givers, but discreetly disposed of it as soon as they were out of sight.

Together guards and prisoners floundered across a deep, wide stream, with water up to their waists, until they located the place where the trail led up the opposite bank. They went through a bamboo forest and arrived at a camp. The mud was still with them as they climbed a hill to the cabin where they were to be housed. They were relieved that it was in a secluded spot where they would be hidden from the stares of the people.

Prof took Lloyd and Sam back to the stream to wash the mud from their shoes and clean up the leech wounds, but by the time they had climbed back, they were as muddy as before. In fact, they watched in fear and trepidation as the girls from the kitchen tried to get up the mud-slick trail with their precious food and hot water to drink. But what a relief—they made it!

18

But the wicked are like the troubled sea, when it cannot rest, whose waters cast up mire and dirt (Isaiah 57:20).

NOVEMBER 25-26

November 25 was another cold, wet day of inactivity. Lloyd and Sam wondered where they were and why the stopover, but it was no good getting uptight and worried.

After a while, Prof came to the cabin with his officer's writing case, from which he took a plastic bag. Their passports and identification papers! He even had a picture of the workers in Laos, though they had no idea where he had obtained it. He questioned Lloyd about his passport. Lloyd tried to make it clear that he was a Canadian.

Why the questions? What was going to happen? Were they nearing Hanoi? There certainly seemed to be an air of expectancy. Prof counted out some money and stuffed it into his pocket.

About four-thirty that afternoon, the word came.

"Hurry! Hurry! We're leaving!"

With the little packing they had to do, there was no delay, and within minutes they were on the way—Prof, a couple of guards, Lloyd, and Sam. But on the way where? They soon came to an encampment with hammocks strung beneath trees.

"Hurry! Hurry!"

They trotted along as fast as they could before the soldiers had time to realize that "enemy" prisoners were going through their camp.

"It's like cycling past a yard with a mean dog," Sam said to Lloyd. "Know how you pedal real fast to get out of range before he can get you? You leave him barking in your dust!"

There was no dust on that trail, but they were soon out of range of the soldiers, leaving nothing but muddy footprints behind them. They passed camouflaged trucks, parked in the brush. Were they going to travel by truck at last? They arrived at a junction and stood waiting by the roadside. A cold rain began to fall, and they pulled their plastic sheets around them like ponchos. People were coming along the trail to join them, soldiers without weapons, a few girls, thirty to forty children.

Trucks rolled up, six-wheelers carrying gasoline, and then other trucks, all camouflaged. People crowded into the trucks. Lloyd and Sam were led along the rutted, muddy road, past dirty muddy trucks, past the jeers and taunts of the people, to the last truck in the line. They climbed in over barrels and chains and settled in as well as they could. Sam's elbows were tied, and he was secured to the truck, but the soldier only looked at Lloyd and shrugged as if he thought Lloyd hadn't the strength to escape even if he wanted to. A third prisoner joined them, a boy in his late teens, thin and weak, shivering so violently his teeth rattled. His eyes were sunken, his skin scaly and dry. He cowered in terror.

"Poor guy!" Lloyd whispered, as the man tried to get into a comfortable position behind the cab. "It would be a kindness to kill him."

Two soldiers climbed in and stood, armed. There were loud unmuffled roars as trucks ahead began to take off. Now their own truck roared after the others, skidding in the deep ruts, slipping and sliding in the mud. The truck jerked and bumped over the rough road and over stream beds. The riders were soaked in the drizzling rain, cold and miserable. Lloyd and Sam could hear the thin man's head thudding against the boards, his low whimpering cries, but they could do nothing to help.

Suddenly the truck stopped, and the driver got out.

"Engine overheating, maybe," Lloyd suggested.

They were ordered out, and they climbed down into ankle-deep mud. A guard led them up a slippery bank, where steps had been made of packing crates, to a big bunker in the hillside. Soldiers arranged some crates and benches for beds.

Lloyd and Sam noticed that the men here were smoking

cigarettes, not the usual water pipes. They tried to talk to them. One man had a guitar and was singing some Vietnamese country and western songs, and Lloyd held out his hand for the guitar.

"May I borrow it?"

In spite of their protests, Lloyd tuned the instrument to suit his ear, and then sang and played a few songs. The soldiers were amused.

As soon as the truck was repaired, they continued their journey. In the dim light, they could make out mountain peaks and cliffs which are characteristic of eastern Laos. As they crossed open and exposed areas, their guards seemed to be keeping a sharp lookout for planes. Once they heard tremendous gas engines roaring to life, followed by the rumble and clank of machines starting out along the road. Tanks?

It was good to be making time on the road to Hanoi. Surely they would be there soon! But it was still night, and they were still in the mountains with no sign of any village nearby, when the truck came to a halt again.

They were so cold, tired, and wet! The night was so dark! Led by Prof, they began to climb a rough road covered with stones, puddles, and rivulets of water. Sam was right behind Prof, then Lloyd, and the young prisoner, "Skinny."

Lloyd was exhausted. "Sam. Slow down! Don't try to go so fast!"

Skinny was exhausted, too. Once or twice he fell face down in the road and lay there in a pitiful heap. Lloyd almost wished he could lie there with him and forget the horror that was around them.

"Get up!" The guard was pulling at their companion, trying to get him on his feet, but he had no strength left. Finally the guard had to pickaback him up the hill. When the road leveled, they came to a few buildings, in one of which was a light. Water was dripping from the thatched roof into a barrel below. Lloyd was so thirsty! He reached for his bowl and dipped it into the water, but the guard grabbed his arms just in time. They were brought hot water to drink and allowed to rest for a time.

As the day dawned, they were taken along a treacherous

forest trail to an encampment by the river. There were only two small buildings, one of tarpaper. People were huddled under little plastic canopies they had rigged up, or lined up outside the kitchen, waiting for food to be dished out. Lloyd and Sam recognized some of the children as those who had been waiting for the trucks the previous night. Apparently they were all in a convoy traveling together.

But they did not eat together. The boys were taken just outside the camp and told to sit on a stack of plastic feed or rice bags. Miserably cold and wet, stinking with dirt and filth, they huddled under their plastic sheets.

"Sam, what day it it?"

Sam thought for a moment. "Sunday."

"Could we sing and pray?"

They tried, but it was not easy to sing that morning. Lloyd looked at Sam. Poor guy; he sure looked miserable! What shame and degradation they were enduring. He remembered the verse about Christ being outside the camp, bearing shame. And here they were, outside the camp, the offscouring of the earth in the eyes of their captors. Yet they were not really prisoners of war, for they had nothing to do with the war raging in southeast Asia; they were prisoners of the gospel. They were here because they represented Christian missions and what the Vietnamese thought of them.

"Sam. Christ is here—with us, outside the camp!"

Sam nodded glumly.

"We share His reproach, but we can share His glory too, now at this moment as we remember Him!" Lloyd said. And suddenly words from *The Messiah* rang in Lloyd's ears— words he had sung with the chorale at Vanier High. "The glory of the Lord shall be revealed; And all flesh shall see it together." There in utter misery, soaked to the skin, he tried to remember the words of that "Hallelujah Chorus." He was too weak and ill to sing the words but he realized that as a representative of "all flesh," he had caught a vision, had a foretaste of the glory of the Lord.

Sam admitted afterward that his own attitude was ungrateful that morning; even the idea of being a heavenbound pilgrim did not appeal to him, but he did come to understand a little better what the Lord Himself had suffered when He lived on earth as a man.

They were hungry and thirsty. Others were being fed. Why were they neglected? Sam pulled out his bowl and waved it, trying to attract attention. At last Prof came and led them to the kitchen building. Welcome warmth! They shed their wraps and tucked into a meal of rice and meat. As a super treat, a soldier mashed cereal bars in a metal cup and poured hot water over them to make a thick, sweet, nutritious concoction. They had as much as they could eat.

Back at the road, they waited in an open-sided warehouse for the trucks to start again. A truck roared to life and they went over to climb aboard. Three men in bamboo-sling stretchers were put in first and lashed into place with their feet at bottom and heads high. Fifteen little children, plastic-wrapped against the rain, got in next; and then came Lloyd, Sam, Skinny, and the four guards. They were so crowded that Sam had to ride in a crouched position. They thumped and bumped over the rough roads, hanging on for dear life, their bodies bruised and aching. Why were they traveling in daylight on an open road? Were they in danger of being bombed?

They traveled for some distance through the mountains before descending into a valley below. The trucks stopped in a lineup, and heavily camouflaged tanks—looking like huge brush piles—rolled by. Everybody was ordered out.

"Where are we?" Sam asked. "In Vietnam?"

"Yes."

"How far to Hanoi?"

"Two days."

Two days! Where had they heard that before?

Now they were walking again along a muddy trail, passing bomb craters forty feet across. When they came to a village, Lloyd and Sam tried the "low profile" idea, and hid their beards and faces behind plastic, but they were soon spotted by the children. All the villagers came out to yell, threaten, and throw mud balls until guards drove them off.

They were taken to an open building in the center of the village and given small stools on which to sit. The people

90

crowded around, pushing at each other to get a better sight of the prisoners. Lloyd and Sam tried to sing, they tried to smile, they tried to talk in Lao—but no one understood. Prof seemed irritated with the people's attitude and moved the boys to a large house with adobe walls and just two or three small barred windows, where it was possible to keep the people away. But the children climbed to the eaves and peered over the walls.

After a drink of hot water and a short time to warm themselves and rest, they had to set out again. Villagers ran along the trail beside them, yelling and screaming. A middle-aged man suddenly stopped in front of Sam and grabbed him by the shirt. His face was ugly. Sam managed to shove him away, and they hurried on through the rain.

That night was spent in a bunker below the ground, dark, low-ceilinged. They crawled onto a wooden platform only a few inches out of the mud. Over their heads were poles covered with plastic sheets which acted as tents to hold out the earth dropping from above.

Because they were hungry, they ate the unappetizing food that was given to them. They slept out of exhaustion.

19

He brought me through the waters; the waters were to the ankles . . . the waters were to the knees . . . the waters were to the loins (Ezekiel 47:3-4).

NOVEMBER 27-28

They awakened early next morning to the distant but steady rhythm of bombing and were given a meager meal of rice and salt. As always, they bowed their heads to give thanks. Their traveling companion, Skinny, had learned to wait for grace before he began and to share his portion with the others. There was no sign of Prof that day, nor did they ever see him again. It was frightening to be in the charge of new guards with whom they had difficulty in communicating.

They soon hit the trail, to repeat the familiar pattern. Only now the villages were more frequent, strung out like never-ending chains along the trail. In every village, people followed, shouting, hurling insults, and threatening. With only one guard apiece, protection was inadequate. At one village, a woman rushed out from the crowd waving a club at them.

"Run!" the guard with Sam said.

Lloyd, who was just ahead, caught sight of Sam loping by him "like an old Clydesdale," and he took the cue and tried to run as well. It was difficult for them both: Lloyd, because of his weakness; and Sam, because of skin eruptions and inflammation which had been caused by dirt and chafing. But fear drove them forward.

The children were the worst. *"Mee! Mee!"** they shrieked, and rushed at them screaming, trying to beat them with sticks. The memory of the fiendish hatred the children showed would always remain with Lloyd as the most disturbing and saddening

_____
*Vietnamese for *American*.

92

memory of the trail. But even while he was repulsed, his heart reached out to them. They were not to blame. They had been brought up with the idea that all the social, moral, and political woes of their country were due to American involvement in southeast Asia. They had been taught to believe that these Americans ate children and raped women! Lloyd and Sam realized that they were seeing the naked face of evil here in a place where the darkness had no comprehension of the Light of the world. What chance had these people against the whole system of evil that was driving them downward, ever away from God, over the brink and into hell? A deep sorrow and compassion began to grip Lloyd, slowly taking the place of the resentment and hatred he had felt in the beginning. He couldn't love his enemies yet, but he could pity and pray for them.

After the day's walk, they came to army quarters just outside a village, where they were taken to a building made of wooden poles and flattened Luong Kho ten-kilo cans. Luong Kho was the trade name of the cereal bars which now and then provided them with a little extra nourishment. This time they received no bars, although they had asked for them. But at least the tins provided protection and kept the crowd outside! Girls from the camp kitchen came with spinach-like greens, fish salt, tiny bits of pork fat and meat, and rice. Skinny ate very fast. Lloyd still had little appetite. The night was cold, and they were one blanket short again because they had left Lloyd's, rain-soaked and heavy, at their previous stop.

The next day they were put in the charge of another group of guards.

"I wonder if they have our papers and watches," Sam said.

"Maybe Prof has gone ahead and taken them to Hanoi."

They were relieved to leave the main trail and follow one which, although vague and undefined, avoided the villages and heavily populated areas. Part of the way they walked along dikes near flooded rice paddies. Water poured through the openings, and here and there over the dikes themselves. Their feet sank deep into the mud below. Even the guards became uncertain of the way. At one point, Skinny went through first, feeling the way with his stick. He stumbled in the cold waters and was soaked to the chest, but managed to reach the other

93

side. Guards took Lloyd and Sam a different route and found water only thigh-deep. Physically weak, Lloyd found that the mud dragged at his feet, and his soaking wet pants added extra weight.

Sam describes that day's going: "We had slugged so far and so much off the trail, and Lloyd and Skinny were worn out. I was healthy, but the cold, the wet, the muddiness bothered me. Over and over I kept saying, 'This is ridiculous.' At times I tried to laugh it off, but I kept wondering why the Lord was putting us through this. It was obviously a patience test, and I wanted to pass it without giving in to frustration."

When they reached a crossing that appeared wider and deeper than before, they stripped and crossed, holding their weapons and clothing high to keep dry. Sam stepped into a deep hole with water to his chest, but managed to keep his things dry. Skinny began to falter. Now and then he fell off the dike and lay in the rice paddy, face down, whimpering in despair. The guard would grab him and pull him out of the shallow water all dripping and muddy, and force him to continue.

They came to the steep edge of a big river. Looking down, they could see a boat landing with several narrow Viet boats with outboards. Curious people from a nearby village gathered, but the guards kept them at a safe distance. As soon as fuel was taken down to the boats, the little group of travelers made their way down the bank to board them. They were soon midstream and moving quickly. Would this river take them to Hanoi?

Lloyd, whose vision was better than Sam's, began to point out items of interest on the way. They could see the pock marks of bomb craters on the hills. They passed two wrecked bridges, only the pylons left standing, a section or two hanging twisted and useless. They saw villages with boats moored on the river below, bamboo and banana trees, even some church buildings. One church had a steeple but no roof. Other boats passed them, some motorized, and others with only a single oar.

Because of their wet clothing, the breeze felt chilly, and

Lloyd and Sam pulled their plastic sheets around them as shelter from rain and blowing spray. They huddled together, each munching on a Luong Kho bar.

After an hour or so of travel on the water, they disembarked on the far side and climbed up the bank to a trail that led into a village. They were taken to a thatched shelter where there was a bed frame, bags of rice, shocks of straw, and some trays. An old woman came in to sweep the floor and tidy up, and soon the crowd began to gather. Because it was a cold blustery day, the people were bundled up: children wore cardigans and hand knitted bonnets and caps; some adults were in Siberian style hats with earflaps. It was all very different from Laos. The children seemed well fed, and there was no evidence of malnutrition. Young adults were in uniform. Older men wore blue jackets and old-fashioned soft campaign hats.

An old man came in and began to lecture the prisoners in Vietnamese, apparently bawling them out; and the crowd laughed and pushed forward, trying to hit them. Lloyd tried speaking in Lao, but he was not understood until an old man who knew the language came forward.

"We are not soldiers," Lloyd explained. "We are teachers of the Jesus religion." The man turned and interperted to the people.

"Are you priests?"

"No, we are not priests, but we teach about Jesus." Lloyd tried to put it as simply as he could.

As the information was passed along, there were murmurs of amazement. The people still crowded close out of curiosity, and the children kept up their peeking and poking, but there was no longer any hostility.

They were fed and given vitamin pills, but it looked as if they were to spend the night in this cold, open shelter. Lloyd began to beg for a warmer place. He pointed to a house nearby.

"Why not there?"

"Full up." But the guards found a woman who seemed willing, and there was a long discussion. "If she will not let you stay in her house, you must sleep out here."

The woman went away and did not return. Sam strung up a hammock, and Lloyd and Skinny got on the bed. But Lloyd felt that he could not stand another night in the cold and wet.

"If I stay out here, I will die!"

Their reply was brutal. "Tough it out."

"If you make me sleep out here, I will get malaria!"

They were given extra blankets and tried to settle down, but such a cold wind blew through the place that it was impossible to keep warm. At last the woman returned, and they were told to pack up and go. They went down a dark uneven trail to a large house, three walls of which were adobe. The fourth was made of two large thatch doors.

How they thanked the Lord for a woman's kindness and for the warm shelter in a cold place! Lloyd and Sam were given a wide split bamboo bed, Skinny a small one. The bed was too short for six-footers, and they had to bend their knees to fit, but they soon settled down for a warm night.

20

Waters shall overflow the hiding place . . . the overflowing scourge shall pass through (Isaiah 28:17-18).

NOVEMBER 29-DECEMBER 3

They were to stay in that village for three days, although they did not know why. They became a sort of menagerie, put on show every day from morning until night, with the guard acting as their keeper to explain to the curious crowd who they were and why they were there. Skinny cowered in fear under his blanket, but men and women would yank it off to peer at him and question him. Most of the time Lloyd was lying down trying to sleep, the blanket over his face. Sam sat up on the outside of the bed so they would look at him and leave the others alone. If and when he did lie down, they came right to the bed to hang over him, wanting him to open his eyes and sit up. He in turn became interested in studying the people, noticing that they did not want to attract attention to themselves, yet they were fearful of the unknown and so very curious that they kept pushing forward. They kept their eyes glued on the strangers.

Even in the dark of the evening when they were trying to sleep, the people crowded around. Sam could hear them and feel their hands pulling at the covers, and he had a feeling of panic. His heart pounded; breathing became difficult. He was seized with a kind of claustrophobia. He sat up suddenly, throwing back the covers, and the crowd moved back.

Lloyd's malaria continued, with fevers at night. Sam was kept awake by his moaning and whimpering and continually asking for water. About this time, Lloyd's feet began to swell.

On December 1, an old man came in from the blowing rain.

He was tall and thin, with a white goatee, dressed in white, and covered by a plastic raincoat. He was clearly a very honorable old gentleman! His manner was friendly and peaceable. He said the name of Jesus and then pointed to himself. Could he be a fellow Christian? He looked at them in love, and their hearts were drawn to him. They could not talk to him, but they were comforted.

From the village they could hear trucks passing on a road some distance away.

"How far to Hanoi?" Sam asked.

"Two days!" said one. Still two days?

"Five hundred kilometers."

Judging from the reports, they were making little progress. Here they were given sweatshirts and pants that were too small. Skinny looked great in his, but the clothes were tight fits for the others.

They had just settled down for their third night in the village when they were suddenly told to hurry and prepare for departure. Girls accompanied them and guided them by holding their sleeves, along a narrow path out of town. It was too dark to distinguish one another, even though they kept close together. They could hear tramping feet going in the other direction, but they could not see the soldiers. They stopped near two trucks. An engined revved up, a horn honked, and they were off again.

Going was rough, but it was good to be moving again. How long did they travel? They had no watches, no way to gauge the time, which could have been from four to six hours. Then they were taken to an adobe house in a small village for the rest of that night and most of the next day.

Few people came to look at them, but those who did were belligerent. A man clouted Lloyd as he lay in bed. An old woman shook her stick at them, and when a guard tried to pull her away, she sat on the sill of the house and waited for an opportunity to strike out at Sam.

That evening they loaded into a truck smaller than those used in the mountains, but it had a canvas cover on the back. A maniac was at the wheel, and they experienced their worst night on the road. The flat bed of the truck dropped out beneath them, then slammed up to send them sprawling. They were soon bruised, blistered, and bleeding. The officer traveling in the back with them could not hold onto his pack, his rifle, and the side of the truck at the same time. Everything and everybody went helter-skeltering around the truck, bashing and bumping everything and everybody else. Every time Lloyd came down with a *wham* on his tailbone, he let out a yelp of pain. Sam tried to land in a squatting position to absorb the bumps more easily. Every time they passed a truck traveling in the opposite direction, the branches of camouflage scraped along the sides of their truck so they were forced to let go. This was sheer torture, but the Vietnamese officer had to endure it, too.

There was nothing they could do to make things easier. They could not sing. They did not want to pray for the truck to stop, because they had hoped and prayed to reach Hanoi. Surely this was faster than walking, and they were spared continuous exposure to villagers. When they finally came to a stop and were able to get out, their legs were like rubber and they could hardly stand. They were taken into a military post to sleep.

December 3 was Sunday, and as their custom, Lloyd and Sam remembered the Lord's death in a simple little service. That day they were well fed, almost more than they could eat: canned luncheon meat, spinach, and soy bean curd with chives or green onion. Their coprisoner, Skinny, was gradually improving in health and spirits and even smiled now and then.

The day began well enough, but word must have reached a nearby village that prisoners were being held in the building, and the people came to torment them. The guards seemed unable to keep any kind of order or afford any protection. The curious crowd tore off the shutters and removed the wall slats so they could toss in pebbles and stones. Surely they were experiencing "the fellowship of His suffering." The words of Psalm 22, so often read in their home assemblies on Sunday mornings, were true of them as well. Men, women, and children surrounded them, staring and yelling like dogs. Some climbed up the opposite side of the wall into the rafters to throw rocks. Some thrust sticks under the partition. Skinny hid under his blanket, weeping, and Lloyd and Sam tried to comfort him.

"O Lord, make the guards send the people away!"

They felt exposed to the taunts and jeers of the crowd like Christian and Faithful in the cage at Vanity Fair in *The Pilgrim's Progress*. One man jumped right over the partition and came at Sam, fists up for a fight. Sam tried to make it clear by pantomime that he was not a soldier and had no desire to fight. But the man pointed to the grenade on his belt and then at Sam.

"O Lord, make the guards send the people away—we can't stand this." Sam prayed again.

"Don't let it bother you, man!" Lloyd spoke from under his blanket.

Sam went over to the bed and tried to force himself to lie there quietly. "But I feel too vulnerable," he said, "especially when pebbles hit me or rocks land nearby."

After several hours, a fine-looking fellow jumped over the partition and began to act as their defender. He had a big stick, and he cracked it at the wall near anyone who dared peer over the partition or throw rocks.

That night the prisoners were too distraught and tense to enjoy the generous supper brought to them. Even the kitchen girls were afraid to come with the meal without soldier escorts.

Lloyd and Sam were offered cigarettes. They pantomimed that they did not smoke, and they tried to show that they would appreciate a banana or an orange. It worked! Somebody got the idea, and hands were extended to them with mandarin oranges. Hostility was over!

As the day drew to a close, the guards came with instructions to pack up and go to the truck. When would they reach Hanoi? Was it still two days or five hundred kilometers away?

21

They have cut off my life in the dungeon, and cast a stone upon me. Waters flowed over mine head (Lamentations 3: 53-54).

DECEMBER 3-6

The pattern of riding for short periods and stopping for longer periods continued. Most of the night of December 3 was spent in a large warehouse which stored crates, boxes, furniture, rice sacks, bricks and lumber. They were locked in and had the place all to themselves, praising the Lord for a good solid building where they would not be molested. They slept on wooden platforms at one end of the building.

Lloyd was suffering from chills followed by fever every night and frequent bouts of diarrhea. He was continually thirsty, and his feet were still puffy. He was only vaguely aware of what was going on around him. Sam was in much better physical condition, and Skinny was still making improvement.

Late in the afternoon of December 4, they boarded the truck again. As it was still light, they were able to see some of the countryside through which they were passing—pleasant farm-lands with many trees along the road. They waited in a lineup of trucks to take a ferry across a river. As darkness fell, the sky gradually cleared, and they could see stars. They were traveling on fairly smooth roads and making good time. Were they nearing Hanoi at last? They could see flashes and hear the faint thuds of explosions in the distance.

Somewhere near midnight, they stopped and were led single file in a big loop, apparently skirting a village. Finally they came to an adobe house. An old women was aroused, and she showed them into a room with two beds.

There were no guards or villagers around when they awakened next morning, but "Granny" was up, tidying and sweeping the main room of the house where her uninvited guests had slept. Sam remembers the room to be about twenty by twenty-five feet, with beds, a table, and some benches. On the wall was a big poster of Ho Chi Minh with happy people all around him, and a few propaganda posters.

At breakfast time, they all crowded into a small cooking area with a tiny fire, trying to get a little warmth. There was one officer, Lloyd, Sam, Skinny, and the granny and grandpa of the house. A metal tripod over the fire supported a pot in which something resembling seaweed was boiling. Grandpa filled a dipper of this bitter tea, poured it into a tiny teapot and then into even tinier cups, and served his guests. This was true Vietnamese hospitality!

They stayed in the house all morning, but when they looked out, they could see bright sunlight and clear blue sky. It had stopped raining for the first time since November 17! They watched their elderly hosts out in the sun spreading rice in small woven trays. Midmorning, girls brought them food, canned luncheon meat, spinach, rice soup for Lloyd because of the diarrhea, and tea.

The rumor of their arrival spread through the village, and the people came, carrying their harvest implements. When the crowd became large, the soldiers drove the people away and closed up the house. It was a sturdy house with bars over the windows, and pegs and bars to fasten the wooden doors, and they felt fairly safe inside despite the persistence of the people on the outside.

Three men came in, and one addressed them in English.
"Stand!"
They stood.
"Names? Nationality? Ages?"
They told him.
"Where captured?"
"Kengkok, Laos."
"How captured?"
"Driving into Kengkok from our home."
"Why?"

102

"We don't know. We did not fight."

"Rank? Unit?"

They explained that they were not in the military but were a carpenter and medic, civilian missionaries.

"You must always call me 'sir'!"

The man's English was clipped and monotone. Sam noticed that he wore a military uniform and had shoes, watch, and pens, which were status symbols. He brought out an old set of handcuffs and clamped it on their wrists.

"You must not react. If you do, you will be shot!"

Was this real? Could it be happening to them? It seemed more like something from an old movie!

They were led out of the house, once more to run the gauntlet between rows of hostile, yelling people. With some difficulty because of the handcuffs, Lloyd and Sam climbed into the back of a jeep and sat on the floor facing the front, with two guards at the sides and Skinny between them. Sam and Lloyd were blindfolded.

"This is ridiculous!" Sam muttered.

"You must not speak!"

They were hot, cramped, and hurting, but the jeep took the bumps better than the trucks. They traveled at speeds which they guessed to be about forty or fifty miles per hour, for fairly long stretches. When it was dark, the blindfolds were removed. Lloyd begged for water continually.

They passed what looked like tanks, and big diesel trucks. They crossed bridges. From the length of the ride and quality of the roads, Sam was sure they were in China! In that one night alone they could have covered the five hundred kilometers mentioned so often.

In the early hours of December 6, the jeep was driven through a narrow passageway and brought to a stop. They were near a plaster building with pillars in front. The North Vietnamese got out their packs and strung hammocks between the pillars.

"You must not speak. If the people know you are here, they will kill you. You must sleep now."

"Please sir, give me some water!" Lloyd begged again.

"We have none."

103

"I must have water—sir!"

The man stringing his hammock over their heads ignored Lloyd's pleas. They tried to sleep, but Lloyd was restless, hot, and irritable with Sam. Handcuffed together, one could not move without the other, and neither could be comfortable. Each blamed the other for his own discomfort. It was a relief when they started out again at dawn.

Although the boys had been blindfolded again, they could tell they were traveling along a busy thoroughfare. They could hear cars, bicycles, and people. Then they entered a quiet street. They heard one gate open, then another. The jeep was maneuvered for parking. People around them were walking. Someone slapped at their legs. Were they in prison now? Would they be put in with other American prisoners of war? They could hear voices and laughter, the repeated ping-pong, ping-pong of a table tennis game, the twanging of musical instruments.

Something warm was thrust into their hands. They felt it, smelt it. Bread! Fresh, warm bread! Happy birthday, and this was better than a birthday cake. Sam was twenty years old that day.

Still blindfolded, they were led stumbling through doors and corridors. They stopped. Blindfolds were removed. For a moment they were blinded by the bright sunlight. Then they saw that they were in a courtyard before an open door. A key was produced, and the handcuffs were removed They were pushed forward into a cell and locked in. They had reached Hanoi at last.

22

I am an ambassador in bonds (Ephesians 6:20).

DECEMBER 6-18

They called it the "Hanoi Hilton," the accommodation with which Lloyd and Sam were provided in Vietnam. But it did not meet the usual luxury appointments and room service of its sister hotels. Their cell, approximately ten feet by ten feet, had no furniture except beds and the ubiquitous bucket. Soon after their arrival, they were each given a big roll containing two new blankets; mosquito net; hand towels; soap; toilet paper; tooth brush and paste; two sets of gray prison garb—of incredible size; maroon and pink striped underclothes; and socks and rubber sandals. They each had a tea jug for tea or hot water.

They changed into the clean clothes. Lloyd took a long drink of the water he had craved for so long, then he sank back on the bed, exhausted. They had expected immediate release. Sam had hoped that he would be starting for home on his birthday—today, December 6. But they were in prison and being treated very much like prisoners, not VIPs. Surely this was only temporary accommodation! Any minute now, a representative of the Canadian government would arrive, and Lloyd would be freed. The North Vietnamese would never keep him here when they realized they had made a mistake in capturing him. But he did not know much about his captors; nor did he realize their indifference to his citizenship, Canadian or otherwise.

Their first meal consisted of a small loaf of bread apiece, soup with noodles and cabbage, a few strings of meat, and a plate with a little white grease. Most of the meals were much the same as the first. Room service was supplied by a number of guards. There was Mr. Cool, who wore civilian clothes and spoke English fairly well, and another they soon began to call "Bear" or "Quickly" because he was irritable and impatient, always ordering them to hurry. After the meal, Sam had to wash the dishes, and then he was taken to a water reservoir, where he washed the few of their travel-worn clothes that were worth saving. He was brought back into a courtyard for a haircut and shave. Lloyd was roused from sleep so his hair could be cut, and he was ordered to shave, but the effort was too much for him.

"You do it. Quickly!" the guard said to Sam.

That was the first thing Sam did for Lloyd there in the prison. But it was only the beginning of his almost continuous care for the next two weeks—days of which Lloyd remembers very little.

Because he was in fairly good health, Sam's lot was to do all the room chores and clean-up jobs. But at least these activities helped to pass the time. He made an attempt to make the cell look more homelike, and put up a string on which he could hang towels and washcloths. With paper wrappings from Luong Kho cereal bars, he tore letters with great care— E M M A N U E L—and used toothpaste to stick them up on the wall over the door. Emmanuel—God with us—because it was December and almost Christmas, and because even in that cell they were sure of His presence.

Whatever he was doing, emptying and washing the bucket, cleaning up the laundry area, or sweeping the courtyard, Sam was urged to haste by the guard's repeated orders, "Quickly! Quickly!" His orders in English were hard to understand, and when Sam did not catch on, he shouted even more loudly and impatiently.

"Bring the tea jugs, quickly, quickly!" And the tea jugs were taken to the door to be filled from galvanized buckets of steaming tea.

When he walked across the courtyard: "Quickly! Quickly!" When he tried to scrub off the soil and grime of the trail: "Quickly! Quickly!"

The guards seemed anxious that the foreigners not be seen by anyone, and they certainly did a good job of keeping them

106

isolated. Lloyd and Sam thought they heard the hacking cough of their trail companion, Skinny, a few times in a cell near them, but they never saw him again.

When they wanted to report anything or to call for help, they were told to use the words, *bow kow*. As soon as Sam realized just how ill Lloyd was, he tried out the strange words. At his request, the guard eventually brought a doctor, who took Lloyd's temperature and blood pressure and examined his feet, now swollen and very puffy. The second day, a doctor and an interpreter came. He asked the boys all the questions that had been put to them so many times since their captivity: name, rank, family, passport number, occupation, circumstances of capture, and so on, and filled in a long, official-looking form. He then proceeded to examine them. Sam was in good shape, but Lloyd could hardly stand, and the edema was not only affecting feet and ankles, but his abdomen was protruding, his face was puffy, and his eyelids were swollen.

The next few days, Lloyd was alternately delirious or in a semi-stupor, and the pills the medic brought seemed to have little effect. Sam tried to rouse him long enough to get him to take a little food, or at least to swallow some of the always-too-salty soup.

Every afternoon, Lloyd and Sam had a daily prayer time. No matter how ill Lloyd was, no matter how confused he had been during the day, talking of rabbits on the bed, pigs in his shoes, or birds flying in and out of the window, when prayer time came, he was clear-headed.

"I can't understand it!" Sam marvelled. "Every day when I wake you to pray, you are as rational as can be!"

Lloyd nodded. "God can do it! That's His special gift to me."

Sam noticed that a little pimple on his foot had changed into a hard blister, and he remembered that the first night in the cell he had been bitten by a tick. It did not look good. If that tick was infected, he'd be in for trouble—tick fever or typhus. But the medic pooh-poohed the idea that it was anything serious.

"That's where your sandal was rubbing," he said.

"It's a tick bite. I could get typhus."

The attendant sneered and turned away.

That evening they could hear a movie projector being set up in a room nearby, and soon the air was filled with the sounds of rifles, machine guns, and bombs, as a war film was shown. Lloyd was delirious—trying to say something again and again, and then falling back in frustration. Sam was frightened, sure that Lloyd would die in the night if he did not get help.

"Bow kow! Bow kow!" Sam yelled, as loudly as he could, but with the noise of the film, nobody heard him. As soon as the movie was over, he began to call again, and Mr. Cool came to the door.

"In the morning the doctor will come. Wait until the morning," he said.

But Sam would not let him go. He followed him, and in the darkness just outside the cell door, he pleaded with the guard.

"My friend is delirious. I know he is just a step away from death. He is a Canadian citizen—not an American—and your country is friendly with Canada. If you let him die in prison without notifying the Canadian government, your country could be embarrassed. I do not want this. Please do something!"

"You are a prisoner. Do not forget this. You cannot pressure us."

"I know I am a prisoner—that I have no rights—that I can't pressure you. But please contact the Canadian authorities about Mr. Oppel!"

"I will speak to the camp authorities," Mr. Cool promised. Sam turned and walked despondently back to his bed.

"Sam, I heard you. Don't worry. God can do it. He'll take care of us," Lloyd whispered.

The next day Lloyd's whole body seemed swollen, and his eyes were almost shut. Two doctors came and poked at the edema, percussed his abdomen and back, listened with a stethoscope to his heart. They promised some medication. Sam tried to talk to them about his infected tick bite, but the only result was some cotton and a syringe needle so he could drain the blister.

After surviving forty days and nights on the Ho Chi Minh

trail, were they to die here in the prison? They had so much faith in the medical help they would get here, and so little was being done! Death was closer to them now than it had been in the cold muddy bunkers and the filthy hooches of the trail.

"We realized deeply our absolute dependence upon God for deliverance," Sam said afterwards. "We could not help ourselves. My medical knowledge was useless without medicine. The North Vietnamese medics weren't properly trained and didn't care about us."

But Lloyd said over and over, "God can do it! God can do it!"

Their first Sunday in prison, there were cereal bars for breakfast as well as tea, bread, and sweet bean soup. Lloyd could not eat, but he roused for a few minutes, and they remembered the Lord together. For the first time since their capture, they had real bread for their communion.

The day was long, and Lloyd was sleeping, so once again Sam resorted to singing—as loudly as he could. The peephole in the prison door opened.

"Be quiet! You must not sing!"

Even Paul and Silas were not forbidden to do that. What could he do with his time, once he had folded the blankets, cleaned the room, tried to remember a passage of Scripture and meditate on it, and repeated all the multiplication tables to fifteen? He looked at Lloyd, trying to picture what he had been like—the sharp looking, fast thinking, alert fellow he once knew. Now he was like a child, helpless and dependent. Sam had to help with everything, even tying the strings on his clothes, covering him at night, and tucking the blankets into the mosquito net.

In his delirium and nightmares, Lloyd talked of being lost and going to hell, about Satan winning victory over God, about fears that he was not saved. His ravings distressed Sam. During the day when Lloyd was rational, he had no such doubts and fears, and together they prayed most earnestly that the nightmarish dreams would not continue.

Seven days after the tick bite, when he expected it would happen, Sam's fever hit. He was burning, restless, aching, and ill, but still he managed to help Lloyd. He was feverish and weak for several days and only able to do small chores in spite of Quickly's insistence that there was nothing the matter and that he was lazy. His gums were sore, too, so that it was difficult to chew anything solid, and the heavily salted soup stung his sore throat.

Lloyd was struggling back to life, the pills and injections causing a little improvement. The edema was subsiding, and his delirium had passed for the time being. Sam's illness had left him despondent and dispirited. He felt that they could not exist much longer under these circumstances. Then, one afternoon as he washed the dishes, the sun broke through the clouds. As if from heaven, a verse came to mind: "Lift up your heads; for your redemption draweth nigh" (Luke 21:28). God was going to deliver them, and soon!

He hurried back to Lloyd with the good news, but Lloyd did not catch his enthusiasm.

"I'm not going to contradict you, but I don't have any indication from the Lord," Lloyd said. "Let's wait and see."

But Sam was sure. Next morning he was folding his clothes and blankets before Lloyd awakened. He took down the mosquito net and the towel line. Everything must be ready. He rolled his things in the rice mat for handing back to the prison authorities. He would not need them anymore!

Lloyd awakened and stared at Sam in his activity. "What are you doing, man?"

"Packing up, getting everything ready. Let me do your things too! We don't want to keep them waiting!"

Lloyd rolled over. "There'll be time enough when they come."

Sam waited for the sound of footsteps crossing the courtyard, for the voice of a Canadian or British diplomat. He thought how surprised the guards would be to see that he had everything packed and was ready to go! Hadn't God given His promise?

But the long hours dragged by, and the day was just like any other. When night came, Sam rolled out his rice mat again, made up his bed, restrung the mosquito net. What had happened? Were they to die in Hanoi after all? Would his family never see him again, never know what happened? He

110

just could not believe that they had made it all the way up the trail only to die of disease in prison. He could not put aside his confidence of their imminent release.

As Sam did the usual chores the next morning, his fever-inflamed throat was even more painful with lumps of self-pity, and his tears dripped into the sink. As usual, Bear kept yelling at him, "Quickly! Quickly!" and Sam hastily wiped away the tears with his sleeve.

Back in the cell, he tried to finish his breakfast drink of cereal bars in hot water, but even that hurt.

"It hurts! It hurts so much!" he cried.

Lloyd got up and came over to where Sam was sitting, putting an arm around his shoulders, trying to comfort him. He did not ask whether it was the pain in the throat or the heartache of disappointment which hurt so much.

When lunch was brought, Lloyd bowed his head to give thanks, but his voice cracked. He and Sam broke down and sobbed together.

"I sat on the end of the plank bed, broken before the Lord, admitting I didn't know what He was going to do with us," Sam recalls. "I entrusted my life to Him and prayed 'not my will, but Thine.' "

Talking it over, they realized that for some reason the prison cell was God's will for them. He would deliver them, but it would be in His time, not theirs. They could see how easy it was to be fooled by one's own thoughts and desires, and that there was danger in dictating to God or even in thinking that *strong* faith is the way out. Simple acceptance of God's will for the present brought subdued and peaceful spirits and the knowledge that whether they lived or died, they were the Lord's and He cared for them.

After dark on the night of December 18, there was the sudden sound of exploding bombs. Sirens screamed; the lights went off. They could hear bombers and high-altitude jets. When a low-flying fighter bomber zoomed over, the whole prison seemed alive with small arms fire. The building shook; plaster and dust were flying. The Americans must be bombing Hanoi! Did they know where the prison was? It was not hit.

111

23

Waters compassed me about, even to the soul . . . the earth with her bars was about me forever (Jonah 2:5-6).

DECEMBER 19-23

Daily life behind thick stone walls and iron bars was dull and monotonous. Lloyd and Sam wished they could write letters to their families in Canada and the United States to tell them what was happening. During his months in Laos, Lloyd had written home regularly, recording in diary-letter his first impressions of the country and his experiences with the Lao people. Here they had neither pens nor paper, and even if supplies had been available, they would not have been allowed to mail letters home or carry home a written record. But some events and happenings were etched on their memories, and Lloyd later recorded some of his experiences as if he were writing from prison. He calls these *Letters on Solitary,* and the first one covers the period of December 19 to December 23, and is headed, "The Closet."

Dear Loved Ones,

To say I was very sick when moved into solitary would be no exaggeration. A red-yellow splotch persisted in front of my left eye. Diarrhoea was frequent, the malarial fever recurred daily, and over all I wondered how I would survive. I can barely remember anything that happened between December 6—our arrival in Hanoi—and December 19.

On the morning of December 19, we were told to assemble the few possessions we had and follow an officer to another section of the prison. I recall much difficulty in carrying my things, for I was extremely weak and near the point of death. My small bundle seemed an immense load.

112

When we arrived at this particular section of the prison, two doors were opened, and I looked into my new home. The whole cell was only seven feet long and perhaps forty inches wide. In it was a plank bed six feet long and thirty-two inches wide. I looked at the officer in amazement.

"What are you putting us here for? We haven't done anything!"

"We're going to study your case," was his only reply, as I was prodded into my cell and the door clanked shut.

Once inside, I had to get on the bed, for the eight inches between the bed and wall were hardly adequate to stand comfortably. In fact, there was so little available space that whenever I had to use the bucket, I had to set it on the bed. I spread out my few belongings and lay back. This little tomb had a very high ceiling with a light bulb that hung down. There was one very high window opposite the door.

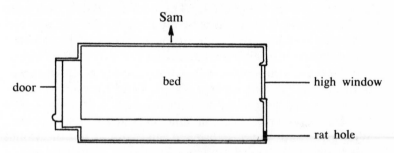

The despair of the situation did not come upon me immediately, but I wondered how I'd survive without Sam's help. After all, he had been assisting me in the most basic functions of life. And yet there was a sense of security in that place, not generated by the confinement, but without a doubt by the comforting presence of the Holy Spirit. Once again I surveyed my bleak surroundings and said aloud, "God can do it!" and fell asleep.

Although I cannot chronologically account for the following four days, some incidents stand out in my mind.

A remarkable thing occurred when I received my first meal in "solo" (as more seasoned POWs referred to it). Previous to this, I'd had no appetite. After contracting malaria twenty days up the trail, any desire for food disappeared, and it was only with great effort that I could force down a small portion of rice or soup. But when I received my first meal in the "closet," my appetite soared, and I ate it to the last morsel with great relish. My stomach rebelled with a class A heartburn, but the full feeling was worth it. I could see God's hand in this, for with the added appetite came sufficient strength to manoeuvre the bucket, get the blankets over me, and dress. On a couple of occasions I even stood on my bed and tried to see out of the high window. There was no view, and after only a moment of this kind of effort, I would be exhausted and fall off to sleep.

Heavy bombing of Hanoi had begun the day before we were put into solitary. Now and then the light would go out in my cell, and I'd have to lie in the darkness. I saved some bread from my meals, and then during the air raids I could chew reassuringly on my little snack. The bombing didn't worry me in the slightest; in fact it was barely audible. But the anti-aircraft gun located close to the prison was a cause for concern when plaster dust fell from the ceiling.

I knew Christmas was not far away, and my great desire was to be united with Sam for that. To that end I prayed. Mustering my strength, I would sit with my back to the thick wall which separated me from Sam and sing out a Christmas carol. With great anticipation I listened, and sure as not, he would sing back.

Despite the seeming helplessness of the situation, I was above the circumstances. Praise the Lord! I feel this was due to the great number of people around the world who were bearing us up before the Lord in prayer.

There was real excitement in my heart as I recalled Christmas at home. If only Sam and I could be together! "If ever I lay eyes on him again I'll embrace him and tell him I love him!" I said to myself, and then the isolation of my cell pressed in on me, and I sat and silently cried.

The rats were bothersome, for they had free access to my quarters through a small hole at floor level, and I had to guard my bread snacks zealously or forfeit them to furry marauders from the sewer.

All in all, the greater part of those four days was spent sleeping, and that, combined with the upswing in my appetite (both these things being possible only by God's grace) accounted for my strength to walk out, unassisted, on December 23 at dusk. Sam and I were reunited without the slightest display of emotion, were blindfolded and then moved to another section of the prison.

We briefly shared our experiences and rejoiced together at the marvelous way God had restored us to a measure of health and strength. Sam told me how he had dreamed of some of our Swiss colleagues in Savannakhet. In his dream, he had been visiting their house and watched a record turning and turning in a player. But he couldn't understand the words of the song because they were in German. And then they came in English:

> It will be worth it all when we see Jesus;
> Life's trials seem so small, when we see Christ.
> One glimpse of His dear face all sorrow will erase
> So bravely run the race till we see Christ.

It was only a dream, but its source was unmistakable—the Holy Spirit of God reminding us that His grace is sufficient.

Lovingly,
In the service of
   the King of kings,
Lloyd

24

Blessed be God . . . who comforteth us in all our tribulation (2 Corinthians 1:3-4).

CHRISTMAS

Because of their blindfolds, Lloyd and Sam could not see where they were being taken when they left their solitary cells, but they heard the opening of a heavy iron door, the thud of a bar sliding into place, the click of a lock. When the blindfolds were removed, they were still in the dark—literally—because of the blackout, but they unrolled their blankets and lay down.

When the lights came on again, they could see they were in a different kind of room. At the ends of the raised platforms or beds on which they were lying was something which looked like stocks. This aroused new fears and doubts in their minds. Why were they here? Was this one way the Vietnamese had of educating their prisoners—putting them into stocks? The stocks made the beds uncomfortably short, and they had to lie in a diagnoal position. They lay there listening to the bombing in Hanoi and comparing notes on what had happened to them in solo.

December 24, Christmas Eve, the two young men tried to get into the Christmas spirit by singing carols to each other; but it was hard to feel enthusiastic. How could there be Christmas here in a Hanoi prison? That evening a very pleasant English-speaking guard came to visit them, and like carolers pictured on Christmas cards, he was carrying a lantern (because all the lights were off). Another guard with him carried something even better—a big round bread basket filled with oranges and plastic bags of treats.

"Merry Christmas! This is from the priest. He couldn't come, but he sent this to you."

"Merry Christmas!" they replied. "Thank you, thank you!"

The boys could hardly wait until the guards had left. All the fun of a bumpy stocking on Christmas morning could not compare to this!

"What's in the bag?"

"Candies—and cookies—and two cigarettes!"

They sampled the candies right away.

"We should keep some for tomorrow," Lloyd said.

"Yes." Sam readily agreed. But the candy was such a temptation in the long night hours.

"Sam! You're eating yours! You won't have anything left!"

"I know. But—"

"But you won't like watching me eat mine when yours is all gone."

They settled down for the night, but were awakened just before midnight.

"What's that?"

"Music! Christmas carols! But where can they be coming from?"

" I don't know," Sam said, "but it sounds like a tape recording being played above us. Or maybe it's coming over the camp radio!"

"But who would have carols? Maybe one of those peace groups from the States? It sounds real homey!"

"Sh! Listen!"

They lay there listening to all the familiar songs of Christmas, and then "Jesus Loves Me," and later still, "I Would Love to Tell You What I Think of Jesus." The boys sang along with that.

"Oh, I would love to tell these people what I think of Jesus," Sam said wistfully. The tape was played again, and enjoyed again, and together they thanked God for this Christmas gift to them.

It was a prison rule that there should be no exercises on a holiday, and Christmas Day was a holiday. The boys began their day with *coffee*, super black and thick, bread, and prayers for the folks at home. That day, many men and women walked by their door, opened the small peephole and looked in.

A surprise Christmas dinner came that afternoon. There was a big bowl of rice and a bowl of meat with lettuce garnish, half a small chicken, a few hunks of pork in a luscious barbecue-like sauce flavored with onion and garlic, and a very small amount of tangerine wine poured into their tin cups. After giving thanks, Sam started in with great gusto, but Lloyd complained of feeling cold. He just could not get warm, and right then warmth was more important than food. He ate some meat and a little rice, and then went to bed to huddle under his blanket. He watched Sam eat, clearing up every drop of the tasty gravy, and turned away.

"Hey, Lloyd, look at this! A carrot in the bottom of the bowl. Want it?"

"Thanks a lot!" Lloyd opened his mouth and down the hatch it went. At once his mouth and throat caught fire, and Sam just stood there, grinning.

"Sam! That was no carrot! That was a hot pepper!"

"But you were cold. I thought it would warm you up!"

"You wait, Samuel Mattix, you just wait! I'll get my revenge!"

But even the pepper failed to warm Lloyd, and he realized he was in for another bout of malaria.

After Christmas, the quality and quantity of food showed a marked deterioration. There was no bread, only rice with a disagreeable burnt taste.

"Why no bread?" they asked the guard.

"The bakery was bombed."

Someone else told them that all the bakers had been evacuated to the country for safety.

There was no bread for six days, and the soup was thinner and even saltier. Perhaps the cooks had been evacuated too, or had gone home for a Christmas vacation. Lloyd had lost his appetite again and never ceased to be surprised at the amount of food Sam could tuck away.

On December 26 there was a big blast, and the lights went out. They did not come on for several days. They heard later that a power house had been hit. During one of the blackouts, Lloyd said, "Sam, stop tickling my feet!"

"I wasn't! You're imagining things— Eek! Something ran across the blankets. Must have been a rat!"

Every night they heard the rats squealing and scampering around. Sam said their cell must be on the rats' main highway—Intercell 5! He discovered that they came in the gutter hole from the outside and across to a hole in the door. Any saved bits of rice or bread had to be guarded or they would disappear in the night.

Occasionally, Lloyd and Sam could hear American voices. Apparently prisoners of war who had just been sent to their section had been part of a larger group, they were calling out names and trying to find where everyone was. The men sounded healthy, alert, and very American. Just hearing their voices was great for the morale of the two missionary prisoners. They heard the men razzing the guards, exchanging jokes, and carrying on some kind of intercell quiz games.

For some reason, Lloyd and Sam never called out to the other prisoners or told them who they were. Sam did sing loudly a few times, but his singing never elicited any response.

The two did a lot of talking during the three weeks they were in the cell with the stocks—to which they were never confined, praise the Lord. They exchanged family histories. They talked about what they would do if and when they returned to Laos, or if they had to stay in America or Canada. They discussed methods of evangelism, the how-to-do-its of Christian work. They reviewed Bible stories and verses from the Bible and prayed.

Several days the weather was very cold, and they wore underclothes, prison garb, sweatshirts—everything they had— and then wrapped themselves in blankets. With continuing attacks of malaria, Lloyd was sometimes very cold and sometimes very hot, soaking his clothes with sweat each night. Sam had to do the washing in frigid water, and then everything was strung up in their cell for the slow process of drying.

Early in January, Lloyd felt much better and had four or five days free of malaria, and then the attacks began again. Sam noticed that the daily exercises were becoming more of an effort for him, and soon he gave them up altogether. He too was experiencing daily attacks of malaria.

For both Lloyd and Sam, January 16 stands out in their memories. Once again they were separated, this time to go through the most difficult period of their imprisonment. Lloyd tells what happened in his second *Letter on Solitary,* which he entitled "Interrogation."

25

O my God, my soul is cast down within me . . . all thy waves and thy billows are gone over me (Psalm 42:6-7).

Dear Loved Ones:

To document my experiences in prison is difficult, for not only must I recall all the triumph, but also the failures—times when I was consumed with hate, times when I was weak, times when I was "neither hot nor cold."

In three brief weeks of solitary, my entire life was reviewed before me. I saw every facet of my own personality exposed and, praise God, I saw that all I had, was, and could ever attain to, was only in Christ Jesus. To this end I pray that I might put off the old man and daily conform to the image of God's own dear Son.

On the morning of January 16, we sat in our cell munching our morning ration of bread, when an officer came and questioned us briefly. Then he told Sam to get his things together; he was moving out.

An icy cold feeling filled the pit of my stomach. I found any new situation a source of great upset, and the thought of our lifestyle being interrupted was hard to accept. Then I reconsidered. Perhaps Sam would be put in with other men! Perhaps he was going home! Perhaps I was going home!

"Fear not, nor be afraid of them."

Moments later I said goodbye to Sam, and he disappeared through the door. I was without human companionship, but not alone. I would have to make the best of things. I'd have to care for myself, and perhaps that additional activity and responsibility would speed my recovery. I was just becoming reconciled to my new state when the same officer returned and told me to get my things together, I would be moving as well. I did not dare ask where, but anticipated something good. When I had rolled up my belongings, I was escorted down a hallway and into the back of a jeep. The great iron gate opened, and we were out in the street. Where were we going? To the airport? But surely I would not need to bring along my things if I were to be released.

I sat back in my seat for fear that I might be spotted by hostile civilians and watched the sights of Hanoi go by. It was an incredible place, bustling with oxcarts, bicycles, trucks, and buses. There were no apparent rules of the road as the driver swung from one side to the other. People were everywhere. I was excited by the chance to see the city, but I noticed evidences of bombing everywhere. We continued through the urban areas and finally reached the outskirts. Perhaps we were going to the airport after all! After about half an hour, we stopped in front of a large iron gate which was quickly opened, and we drove inside. I unloaded my things and was taken through hallways and room until we came to a large cell. I entered—and was left alone.

I looked around. I had never been in a place like this before, with room to move around! There was a water tank, chair, table, and bed. I would be able to eat my meals at a table instead of on a bed. Civilization at last!

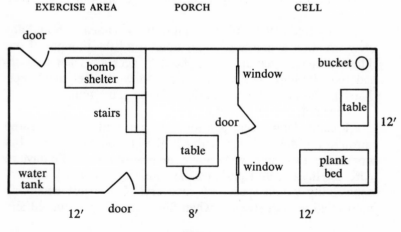

By prison standards, things were quite nice, what with a twelve-by-thirty-two-foot area to myself. There was even a partly enclosed hole for a bomb shelter, but that wouldn't have done me much good, as I was locked in my cell room at least fifteen hours a day.

To be in such comparatively palatial surroundings made me nervous. Was this treatment to be used as an incentive to make me cooperate? I had noticed other prisoners, Vietnamese, relatively free inside the prison doing chores or sitting at tables, writing, and surmised this was an indoctrination centre.

After lunch, a man who spoke English, and who later turned out to be my interrogator, came into the cell and gave me the Seiko watch which had been taken from me on the day of capture! I put it on my now emaciated wrist, and it slid three-quarters of the way to my elbow. Now I knew what time and day it was, although I have no more than a vague recollection of the sequence of events during the following three weeks.

The first few days passed without incident. The weather was cool, and I was wearing all I had and was asking for more.

"Please sir, may I have a sweater?"

"We are working on it!"

"Please sir, may I have quinine? I have malaria."

They were working on that too, but both were slow in arriving. Perhaps I should describe a malaria attack so you can appreciate how I spent six to eight hours of every day. First came the chills. They always started with a little shiver and would progress until I felt refrigerated and my body would twitch and convulse. I would rub myself to try to generate heat. When it seemed I had reached the limit of my endurance, the chills would subside and I would begin to warm up. What a wonderful feeling! But then I couldn't turn the heat off. I would push off my blankets, take off my clothes, and toss and turn. This would keep up for a couple of hours until I was totally exhausted and, head and heart pounding, I would lie back with the weakness of death upon me and fall into a heavy sleep. After several hours I would awaken, drenched in sweat, and thirsty, so very thirsty. Taking my teapot, I would savor a mouthful of Dunlop tea—a unique prison beverage with the distinct flavor of rubber tire.

123

It was not unusual for me to awaken in the night, and since the lights were always on, I could survey my surroundings. Sometimes I would see a face peering at me through the little window in the door. Most of the guards were young fellows, and I guess zealous in measuring up to their responsibility. One I saw frequently not only carried his carbine rifle but also had the bayonet in place. These fellows were as curious as had been their counterparts on the trail. They'd come into my cell and rummage through my possessions, and even try to converse with me, although I knew no Vietnamese.

After some days, I was taken from my cell to a nearby room for interrogation. The first session was about three hours long and was comprised mostly of questions, one man questioning and another taking notes. Both spoke English acceptably, and one appeared well versed in foreign affairs.

At first these sessions were somewhat welcome. I had someone to talk to, something to do. But as time progressed, they became burdensome indeed; the long hours of incessant questioning, the pages of essays, and the continued regurgitation of facts were odious. The papers I had when captured (passport, birth and health certificates, letter of guarantee from Christian Missions in Many Lands, and other documents) were shown to me, and I had to explain them and write essays about them, including every entry in my passport. The detail was absurd. When they discovered I had spent time in the States, I was told to write a detailed report on those three months, noting everyone I had stayed with, every place I had been, what affiliation I had with the military. Then would come the inevitable question: "Why did President Nixon send you over here?"

And so it went, until my mind began to swim from the effort of trying to reconstruct twenty years of life on paper.

After many sessions of interrogation, they seemed prepared to believe I was a Canadian. In view of this, I tried to reinforce my position as a neutral, insisting that there was no good reason for my detention.

Finally the reason for my captivity was given: "You see, Mr. Oppel, in southeast Asia there is a war with a front line, and you happened to be on the wrong side of that line."

I went back to my cell convinced that my nationality would

afford me no unique status. How long would I be here? I knew prisoners had been taken back in '68, and some Christian and Missionary Alliance folk as early as '63. As I contemplated long-term imprisonment, my spirits sank deep into the valley of depression. I might not get out until I was twenty-six or twenty-seven years old. The world would have changed. Perhaps my parents would be dead. After all, Dad was already seventy-two. My eyes stung, but no tears came. The thought of never seeing my father again hurt incredibly. Oh, no, not five years! What's it like after a year passes and there is no release? Then two years, three, and then five and still nothing. The fear was paralyzing, the despair hard to bear.

My prayer life at that point took on an added dimension. I was not begging God for release. After all, He had brought me here, and He would get me out. But I needed to pray more earnestly for my own life and relationship to God, and most of all, for others. It wasn't easy, I assure you. I wanted to run away like a small wounded boy and bury my face in my mother's apron. But I learned a very important lesson I trust I shall never forget. When the burden seems too heavy and I want to run away—to cop out—it isn't time for a holiday, or to kick up my heels, or to go to sleep and forget it all. It isn't even time to take two aspirins and rest in bed! It's high time to get on my knees. Morning and afternoon I sat on my plank bed in the cell, enshrouded in a blanket, and with great concentration bore up my loved ones before the Lord. Carefully I envisioned the Sunday morning congregation at home, and one by one I asked God's best for their lives. Daily I asked healing for the sick, growth for the weak, joy for the sorrowful. I was still deep in the valley, but not alone.

About this time one day, a guard came to my cell carrying a syringe and an assortment of vials.

"Quinine?" I asked, pointing at the medicine and hoping here at last was an answer to my numerous requests.

"OK," he replied, utilizing his entire English vocabulary.

I believed him, and from then on I received daily injections of an assortment of liquids. Often the needle was dull, and penetrating my vein was extremely difficult. The veins stood out in bold relief on my thin arm, but did not seem well enough anchored for him to puncture with his dull needle.

After these injections were started, I began to dream frequently and to hallucinate. My nighttime fantasies carried over and became daytime realities. Unlike the delirium that came with the fever which brought nightmares I cannot remember, I have total recall of the hallucinations I experienced during this time.

One afternoon, I lay down for a nap and began to dream. My mind soared into the universe, and I beheld all creation. From my vantage point, I saw something most incredible: for everything that existed there was an identical duplicate! Nothing was unique. If all created things were not unique, then neither was God. He could not be infinite! The universe was a farce! I saw a huge wooden cube, which I divided in sequence until I was left with a minute fragment. This I divided in half, and poof! I had discovered the infinite. I awoke, and the conviction that I had discovered God, or to be more exact, that I had "found Him out," was as real as the food I sat down to eat. I couldn't stand it. I could not tolerate a Godless universe. What a dilemma! I was God.

Admittedly this was pretty far out, in fact totally absurd. But it was what I experienced. To me, this was reality.

I was so depressed by my discovery that I returned to bed, fell asleep, and soon resumed the same dream. Only this time something went haywire, and I wasn't God anymore, and the universe wasn't a farce. I woke up. Everything was back to normal, but the recollection of the experience would not leave me. It seemed that I was losing control of my mind, but I refused to let go.

Another afternoon, I sat in my chair holding "the king" on my lap. Affectionately I embraced "his majesty," informing the guard (who did not exist either) that he should take note of whose lap the king was sitting on, and since he and I were obviously such close friends, I should receive better treatment and additional food. Cradling him, I looked at my arms. They were extended around emptiness! With an effort I released my grip, becoming conscious that neither king nor guard existed. The experience was shattering! As the injections continued, so

126

did the hallucinatory experiences—and so did the interrogations.

As I said, interrogation was burdensome, especially in view of my weakened condition. During this time, the questioning became very pertinent. They wanted names, addresses, and descriptions of my colleagues, relatives, friends, and even Lao Christians. I wanted to be silent. I wanted to be the hero who stood fast and never uttered a word. But I felt intimidated, afraid of consequences if I resisted, totally at their mercy. It was a most overpowering feeling. And so they got the information they wanted, every jot and tittle.

I returned to my cell, and it hit me. Lloyd, what have you done? I cannot describe how I felt—ashamed, broken-hearted, incredibly guilty. I had actually betrayed the people I loved most without the slightest resistance. I was no Geoffrey Bull. I was less than a man. I hated myself. I cried out to the Lord to destroy everything written, to erase every word from their minds. I prayed the same prayer over and over. I went to bed in a stupor of guilt, determined that if I ever got out of prison, I would contact every person I had mentioned, and beg his forgiveness.

I went to sleep a lonely man.

The following morning was as gloomy as my own soul. I sat, but I could not pray.

"And we know"—the words in my mind seemed vaguely familiar. "And we know—" I struggled. "—that all things—" It was coming to me with freshness, as though I had never heard it before! "And we know that all things work together for good—" What a promise! I sought to recall the remainder of the verse. "And we know that all things work together for good to them that love God—" The word "love" sank deep into my guilty soul. "And we know that all things work together for good to them that love God, to them who are the called according to his purpose." Blessed be the name of the Lord!

There in that bleak solitude, God let loose the floodgates, and His blessed forgiveness once more flowed over my soul.

With February came Tet, the Vietnamese New Year. Interrogations ended. One morning I learned that the treaty had been signed. A young guard came in, obviously excited. He was a good looking fellow, always polite, always smiling; but on this day, he was ecstatic. He was jabbering incessantly, and of course I couldn't understand a word. He took his pen and a piece of toilet paper, sketched a picture of the globe, and then, pointing to Vietnam and North America, kept saying, "Go home, go home." That much I understood. It sounded good, but I could not let myself go. When I failed to respond with glee, he insisted, and finally I threw my arms in the air and did a feeble little dance. He left satisfied, and I went to bed as skeptical as ever. However, no matter how I tried to discredit the news, secretly it was very precious to me. From that day on, time passed very slowly.

The three weeks of interrogation were by no means a total loss. I not only found out how pathetic I was, but how faithful God is. And I found opportunity to speak and write of my Lord. Let me give you one of many examples. When asked what I was doing in Laos, the answer I gave was twofold: I was there to help the people physically, which has limited benefit, and to help them spiritually by showing them the way to peace with God. I presented the gospel orally and then wrote it out in greater detail in an essay. This essay was subsequently translated into Vietnamese. The precious seed was sown in weakness, at times in misery, but praise God, the One who brings forth the harvest was in no way restricted by my infirmity.

With Tet also came a celebration, and for a change, some decent food. Previously I had been getting only starchy soup with the occasional bit of bone. One day it was a jawbone complete with teeth—an old pig's dentures and not particularly appetising. But the gums were tender, so I ate them. But at New Year's I got bananas, boiled rice, and soup with meat. What a treat!

By this time, my hair was getting shaggy. It was last butchered in December, and without a comb, it was looking rather bad. My friendly injection-giver came in with scissors and began to display his prowess as a barber at the expense of my unwashed locks. I was told to shave, and I did, leaving behind the shadow of a mustache. Facial hair was against camp rules, but I wanted to grow mine back as a symbol of resistance—which is a good thing to have when there has been no resistance at all.

February 6 rolled around. It was my twenty-first birthday, and we had been in Hanoi two months. I sat on my chair that bleak morning, sang happy birthday to myself, and expected God to provide the present.

He did.

Lovingly,
In the service of
the King of kings,
Lloyd

26

Oh, that my words were now written (Job 19:23).

Sam and Lloyd did not see each other during their three weeks in solitary, but they were put into similar cells and shared much the same treatment. Every day Sam had chills and then fever as the malaria followed its regular cycle, and although a kindly guard brought him a new sweatshirt, a quilted vest and two heavy but dirty blankets, he could not get warm when the chills came on.

Interrogation sessions for Sam began early in the morning, sometimes before breakfast. As well as being asked oral questions, he was given a book of questions which required written answers, a task which kept him occupied for several hours.. On one occasion he found there was plenty of paper left over and decided to add a postscript.

"Perhaps you wonder why God led me to Laos, only to be captured. Perhaps you do not believe in God, but I believe that God let me be captured in order to tell you what God wants you to know," he wrote. Then he gave a lengthy presentation of the gospel, keeping the language as simple as possible. He described man's condition, his need of God, and told of God's love in giving His Son to die on the cross.

The next time he was interrogated, he noticed that the questioner was holding the papers he had written.

"You made a mistake!" he said.

"I tried to tell the truth!" Sam assured him. "Show me the mistake."

The man pointed to a place where Sam had repeated a phrase. It was in the gospel section of the paper! Yes, Sam had written the same words twice by mistake, but that error was the means of assuring him that the whole paper had been read.

On one occasion, Sam's questionnaire went something like this:

1. Tell about Mr. Chopard's work and his connection with the government.
2. Tell about Christian Missions in Many Lands: what it does, how it is organized and financed, and what is its connection with the government.
3. Tell about Campus Crusade (same as above).
4. Tell about Christian and Missionary Alliance (same as above).

Following this were questions on what he thought of Lao people, of the Vietnamese people, and of the war in southeast Asia.

"These interrogators sure ask for it!" Sam said to himself as he explained in great detail the familiar message contained in the *Four Spiritual Laws* booklet used by Campus Crusade for Christ.

Better food at the New Year celebration brought a respite, and then came news that the war was over and they would soon be going home. Sam was excited and happy at first, but the days dragged by, and the fever attacks were even more severe and affected his heart. He felt forlorn and forgotten. A tiny blood vessel in his left eye burst, causing a blind spot in his vision.

On February 6, he remembered it was Lloyd's birthday. On Sam's birthday, they had arrived at Hanoi. Would something special happen today? After an unappetizing breakfast of bread and water, Sam sang "Happy Birthday" as loudly as he could. There was a response!

A little later, Lloyd was brought into his cell, and they were taken out to a jeep. Sam's heart was pounding so rapidly and irregularly, he wondered what would happen, but he was even more concerned about Lloyd, who "looked terrible! face yellow, thin, and he seemed sort of half there."

The friendly guard who had been their interrogator shook their hands, and they were off. Would they be released today? Were they going home?

131

27

Cast thy bread upon the waters, for thou shalt find it after many days (Ecclesiastes 11:1).

During the months that Lloyd and Sam had been in Hanoi, they had been together in one cell or in solitary confinement in adjoining cells. They had heard voices, but they had not seen any American prisoners of war. How different their experiences had been from what they had confidently anticipated on that October morning when they set out on the Ho Chi Minh trail! At that time, the prospect of being prisoners for Christ's sake had seemed exciting. Surely the Lord had His purposes in their captivity, and they would be given opportunities to witness for Him, to be His ambassadors in bonds. But apart from what they had written on their interrogation papers, these opportunities had not come. Now, as they left their small prison, their thoughts turned toward release—the prospect of freedom in their own land and the joy of reunion with family and friends.

As the jeep shuttled them once again in the direction of the city, they could see evidences of bomb damage on every side—water-filled craters in the fields, wrecked railway cars on the tracks, and piles of rubble on the streets. People were busy at work with shovels and wheelbarrows. They drove past the hospital, the railway station, and the embassies with their flags flying, arriving once again at Hao Lo Prison, the notorious Hanoi Hilton. Lloyd and Sam could clearly see the ten-foot stone walls topped with jagged broken glass and the eight bare electric wires strung above them. The big iron-barred gates swung open, and the jeep drove slowly through the entrance and into the courtyard. How long would they have to wait? Would they leave for the airport immediately?

132

They caught sight of the familiar face of Mr. Cool, and he came over to greet them. American POWs watched them from a nearby doorway. Lines of familiar prison garb hung out to dry. Sam and Lloyd picked up their bedrolls and tea jugs and followed a guard through the familiar passages to the door of a cell block. The door was unlocked, and they went inside. There, standing to greet them, were eight American prisoners of war!

For a moment they stared at each other, the two missionaries who had not seen a fellow countryman since October 27, and the eight military prisoners. Then suddenly, smiles broke out, hands were outstretched.

"Welcome!"

"We're glad you're with us!"

"I'm Walt!"

"I'm Ernie!"

"I'm Lloyd Oppel from Canada."

"My name is Sam Mattix. I'm from Centralia, Washington."

"Welcome, Lloyd and Sam!"

Were they ever glad to see these Americans, middle-aged or young, fair haired or dark—Norm, Chuck, Jim, Jack, "JR," and Steven! But, coming straight from three weeks of solitary, the voices, the smiles, the questions with everybody talking at once, were confusing and unreal.

"Why did they capture you if you're missionaries?"

They told how the North Vietnamese Army had come into Kengkok and taken over their area, and they were caught behind the lines.

"Sure, they'd capture missionaries! That's the way they are!" It was soon evident that these men were not going to be surprised at anything Lloyd and Sam could tell them.

"Where have you been now?"

"We've just come from a small prison in the country," Sam told them. "We're just out of three weeks solitary." He paused, and the men nodded sympathetically as if they knew just what he meant. "Guess you probably know all about solitary?"

"You see Ernie over there? He's been solo for four years and seven months."

"The Snake Pit," they called it, the cell block into which

CELL BLOCK
The Snake Pit

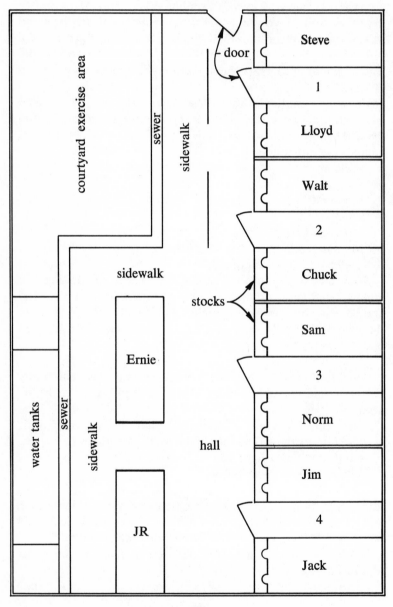

Lloyd and Sam had been welcomed. It consisted of four cells along one wall, two beds (the kind with stocks) in each cell. Just outside was a hallway and small exercise area where they ate most of their meals. A courtyard with water tanks to one side made up the remainder of their block. Two new men now created a problem—they were two beds short! And the newcomers would have to be given the best facilities! Lloyd and Sam had already spent plenty of time together, so Lloyd went with Steve, and Sam with Norm.

When the guard came with food, he was told that two more bed boards and some saw horses would be needed. JR and Ernie, who had volunteered to sleep in the large room, set to work on constructing their new beds while the others dished out the food.

There was no change in the Hilton's bill of fare, Lloyd noticed: cabbage soup, plates of cauliflower with bits of pork fat, loaves of bread.

"Give the meat to Lloyd and Sam. They need it!"

They took their bowls out to the courtyard and sat on the curb, eating and talking. Lloyd and Sam felt a little nervous and strange, coming into this closely-knit group of prisoners. But this did not hinder them from asking the question of most importance to them.

"How soon are we going home?"

"Who knows?"

"It's supposed to be within sixty days," one of the men explained. "There are to be four releases, we're told. One about February 12, another on February 27 or 28, the next mid-March, and the last end of March."

"But—but—I don't get it. Isn't the war over?"

"That's right."

"Why do we have to wait?"

That was a question no one could answer.

Before lunch was over, Lloyd's malaria attack came on, and he began to shiver. One of the men found a cardigan sweater for him.

"We'll see that he gets some medicine," he said. "We'll get him in shape. You should have seen Jack when he arrived, sick and skinny after being on the trail."

Lloyd went to lie down, and as soon as the others had finished washing the dishes, they were locked into their cells until afternoon tea break. Sam soon wearied of talking and fell asleep.

Now Lloyd and Sam had to fit into a regular pattern of prison life which involved others. Tea and bread were brought each day at 6:45 A.M., and from then until lunch time, the men were permitted out of their cells. The time was spent in pacing, sweeping, playing card games or chess, reading, talking, or just thinking. There were a few books and magazines available, *Field and Stream, Sports Illustrated,* some communist propaganda magazines, a few books in English written by Americans critical of US involvement in Vietnam, Russian novels, and technical books. For want of better reading, they read everything they could lay their hands on.

As lunch time neared, someone set out the bowls and plates on the serving board (hardly a table), the bolt was slidden back with a bang, and the door was swung open.

"Eat!" the guard said.

Two men went for the bucket of soup and the basket of bread. Tea came in the afternoon, and the supper meal—same menu as lunch—at four P.M. The only variety in the menu was whether it was with or without meat. With meat was considered an indication that progress was being made in the signing of the peace treaty, and they would be going home soon. Without meat? Probably signing was off, and they would be stuck where they were for a long time.

For several reasons, the adjustment to this new form of prison life proved difficult for both Lloyd and Sam. They were now with a group of military men who had come to fight knowing that they faced the danger of being shot down in enemy territory, men who were in some measure prepared for imprisonment. Some had faced long periods of solitary and interrogation, some had been tortured. They were strong and tough and hard. They were seasoned to prison life and knew the run of the ropes. Like big brothers, they gathered in the two young missionaries.

Lloyd was very weak and still suffering from attacks of malaria. The strain of solitary had taken a greater toll than he had realized. When the prospects of being released and going home were suddenly snatched away and he was faced with the possibility of being in prison for many weeks more, he slid into a slough of despondency and depression. Alone in that cell, he had been dependent upon God. But now, with people around him, he had difficulty reaching out to God. He felt reluctant to pray. And Sam, though not physically as weak as Lloyd, found himself confused and not quite able to cope with this new group situation. He felt self-conscious about going into his cell to pray alone. He and Lloyd, who had been so close a few weeks before, found themselves no longer in need of each other. They knew this would affect their Christian testimony.

Things were already happening right in that cell block to make them realize that it was God's will and purpose for them to be there. First, there was the discovery that they were not the only Christians. The very first afternoon, when they were released from their cells for a time, Jack asked Lloyd, "Can you quote the Twenty-third Psalm?"

Lloyd and Sam began together. "The LORD is my shepherd, I shall not want," and were able to go all the way through.

Jack sat on the edge of the bed, drinking in the words as if they were cold waters to a thirsty soul.

"I have been trying to remember them for two years!" he said. "Do you know any more verses from the Bible?"

They quoted as many as they could.

Later, Jack told Lloyd his story. He was an aeronautical engineer, twenty-six years old, and had been flying over Laos when he was shot down and taken captive. Twice he had escaped from his captors; on one occasion he had been in the jungle for ten days and had come to within about seventy miles of freedom when he inadvertently walked into a North Vietnamese camp. After that, he had been securely tied.

During the long, weary days on the Ho Chi Minh trail, Jack had come to the realization that something was definitely lacking in his life, and he cried to God for help. But he knew so little about God and His Word. Part of the Twenty-third Psalm, verses he had memorized as a child, came back to him. But there was only one verse he could remember in its entirety:

"For God so loved the world, that he gave his only begotten Son, that whosoever believeth in him should not perish, but have everlasting life." Right there on the trail, Jack had put his faith in those words.

"God, it is all I know. Please save me on the basis of that verse." He knew that God had heard his prayer, that a change had come into his life, and now he wanted to find out more about God. For two years he had been looking, hoping that somehow he could find a Bible or someone to tell him more.

On the fifth of February that year (1973), he was feeling low and depressed. He even began to doubt what had happened that day on the trail.

"Lord, I am at the end of my rope," he prayed. "Couldn't You do something just to show that You do care for me, even if it is just something a little different on my tray, or something to read?"

The next morning, he prayed that way again. It was not long before the door opened, and in came Lloyd and Sam. He did not know who they were, but in that instant he knew they were God's answer to his prayer.

On the first Saturday that Lloyd and Sam were in the cell block, JR—who, incidentally, had found that his home town was not far from Sam's in Washington State—talked to the newcomers.

"It's Sunday tomorrow. You two are missionaries. Will you give a church service?"

"Sure."

They decided on the time—after tea in the morning. Jim and Jack took charge of the songs and tried to write out words on toilet paper and cigarette wrappers. They also wrote out the Apostles' Creed. Lloyd and Sam gave the message. It was hardly the Episcopalian order of service to which Jim was accustomed, and it was somewhat disorganized, but it was very hearty. And it was the beginning of regular Sunday morning services.

The very next morning, Sam went to Lloyd's cell with a burden on his heart and the realization that they must put things right between them if they were to be effective in their Christian witness in the block. They talked and prayed together and agreed that they would meet for prayer every day just as they had always done. They set the time at nine A.M. Soon Jack asked if he could join in the prayer meetings, and then Jim.

As they talked to their cellmates in the evenings, or paced up and down the exercise area with them, Lloyd and Sam heard the stories of how these men came to be together in prison.

"As we heard their stories, we felt as if we were among the 'living dead,' " Sam says. "These men were all MIA [missing in action], and their families and friends did not know they were alive. They had survived their crashes and subsequent experiences against high, even fantastic odds. They were being held in Hanoi by the North Vietnamese, while their captors denied and concealed their very existence, insisting they were prisoners of the Pathet Lao [Lao Patriotic Front]. At least, other prisoners occasionally received mail from home. These men did not. Other prisoners might be named by Hanoi on POW lists. These men were not."

Including Lloyd and Sam, they were the only ten prisoners from Laos. Yet 316 were listed as missing in action there. No wonder they were drawn close together and developed a strong sense of loyalty and camaraderie. The eight POWs welcomed the two missionaries to what Ernie called LULU—Legendary Union of Laotian Unfortunates.

28

As rivers of water in a dry place, as the shadow of a great rock in a weary land (Isaiah 32:2).

Every now and then the men from the Snake Pit were allowed to go to the large courtyard near the gate, where they joined other prisoners for some form of entertainment. One night it was a concert given by the Vitenamese Army band, orchestra and dance group which traveled to perform for their own troops. On other occasions they saw films, cartoons, newsreels, puppet shows, and war movies. At first there was strict enforcement of the rule of no communication between the LULU group and other prisoners, but this gradually broke down.

On the morning of February 23, a rumor came from Colonel Guy's group that a treaty had been signed in Laos. A little later, the camp commandant, a thin, nervous, chain-smoking man, and his interpreter came to the cell block, followed by several men wearing civilian clothes and carrying movie cameras. The prisoners were ordered to get into their long clothes—the gray pajamas. When they had reassembled, the commandant put on a pleasant on-camera smile and began to speak.

"I have a most important announcement for you today. When I tell it to you, you will be very, very happy," he said in Vietnamese, and paused for his assistant to interpret, as cameras whirred. "This is the announcement. On February 22, 1973, a treaty was signed in Laos, ending the war. You will be permitted to return home!"

The men of LULU stood there, stolid and expressionless. They had previously agreed that they would not perform for any Viet newsreels.

"You may now clap!" the interpreter told them.

Politely, soberly, they clapped an unenthusiastic time or two, while the commandant and his assistant clapped furious sound effects for the recording.

"Are there any questions?"

Walt, who as senior officer took the position of the group's leader, stepped forward.

"Yes, sir. Will we get copies of the treaty?"

"They are being typed up."

"How soon will we go home?" was Walt's next question.

No answer.

"May we write letters home now?"

"Yes."

"When do we get our Red Cross packages?"

"Sooner or later."

Sam leaned over and whispered something to Walt and he nodded.

"There are two missionaries in our group. They would like a Bible to read. Will you give them a Bible?"

The interpreter and commandant conferred for a moment or two.

"Yes, I will see that one is brought for them."

Yes? They could not believe it! Always the reply to their requests had been, "Sooner or later." Even if a Bible were available, they would probably forget about it. Walt went on asking for milk and special food for Lloyd, and for more free time out of the cells.

The next morning a guard entered and placed a little book on the window cell. The POWs pounced to see what it was. A Bible! A brand new Gideon New Testament with Psalms and Proverbs. They passed it around, handling it almost reverently, so that everyone could see it. Someone read off the contents—the titles of hymns, the list of helpful Scriptures for special times of need.

When they all had taken a good look at the precious little book, Jim, Jack, Lloyd, and Sam went into Lloyd's cell for a praise and thanksgiving meeting. They had had so many prayer meetings to make their requests and petitions, now they could only praise the Lord! They read a chapter together.

141

Of course, everybody wanted to read the New Testament, and everybody wanted to be polite enough to let the other fellow have a turn. For two weeks, that little book was read practically nonstop. One person would read for an hour or two, then pass it on. Several read it all the way through and then started in again. Sam was often called upon to explain words in the King James Version. Especially for those with little experience in Bible reading, he wished they could have a modern English translation. But at least they had a Bible!

The Gideon New Testament issued to the prisoners. Signatures of the men in LULU are shown on the flyleaf.

From that time on, there was a definite improvement in the Sunday services. For one thing, they had words of several familiar hymns. And they had the Scriptures to read and study from when preparing the message. One morning Lloyd spoke on Psalm 103, and Sam chose John 13 when his turn came.

Being able to read the Bible and study the teachings of Christ and His disciples was beginning to have an effect upon Jim. He had been raised in the church and let the church do all his thinking for him, never reading the Word of God for himself. Now he found out how the early church had come into being, and how the Christians gathered to break bread. When on Sunday mornings Lloyd, Sam, and Jack had their simple little communion service using bread and tea, Jim had

142

held back. Surely it could not be right to do this without an ordained priest, and yet, as he read and reread the story, he learned that the disciples themselves were ordinary working men, not graduates from any seminary. And he joined the others as they remembered the Lord's death.

The New Testament gave the men something to talk about and discuss, an interest far away and beyond their limited prison environment. And how they loved to sing! Jack never had enough of it and was eager to learn the words of new songs. He could sing "He's Everything to Me" and really mean it! The prisoners sang "I Looked for Love," and knew that in a prison cell they had love; they sang "They'll Know We Are Christians· by our Love," and sensed the bond which joins those who are one in Christ Jesus. The cell rang with "Happiness Is the Lord," and "I've Got Confidence."

They had the Bible promised by the camp commandant, but there had been no further developments with regard to going home. Early morning broadcasts on Radio Hanoi gave ranting reports of continued US bombing in Laos and of South Vietnamese treaty violations, and hopes plummeted downward.

Then one morning early in March, Lloyd was told to get ready to move. Was he—the Canadian—to go and leave the others behind? He tells the story in his third *Letter on Solitary*. This one is entitled, "The Cure."

29

For my sighing cometh before I eat, and my roarings are poured out like the waters (Job 3:24).

Loved Ones:

It was the beginning of another usual day. I lay there watching with envy as Steve did his calisthenics. When he finished, I did mine—three push-ups and ten sit-ups. It was such a tremendous strain that I lay back panting, my face beet red.

The guard came and unlocked us from our cells, and we were free to mix. Brushing my teeth and straightening my bed were my big preoccupations. Suddenly a guard entered the Snake Pit.

"Loi!"

The others alerted me that my name was being called.

"Get things together, you go!"

"He go where?" Steve queried excitedly. "He go home?"

The guard nodded vaguely. Spirits soared. We had heard recently that Marc Cayer, the other Canadian POW, had been released, so we anticipated that at last my earthly citizenship would be of some good. The others crowded around questioning the unresponsive guard, while Steve helped me take down my mosquito net and roll up my things.

"What about the list, Steve?"

The list was a piece of toilet paper on which I had written the names and nearest of kin of other members of LULU, just in case being a Canadian should afford me an early release. I was so skeptical about any preferential treatment that I had failed to memorize the vital statistics on the list. Now that I was leaving, I would have to carry it with me, but where? My underwear was loose, and it might fall out. The guard told me to "move it." Hastily I pushed the list into my sock and stepped out of my cell. The others gathered close around. At that precise moment, a most unusual feeling came over me. I was saying goodbye to men who had been prisoners for years and who still had a limited prospect of release. I felt unworthy, but they were happy for me. In turn, I shook their hands, and there were wishes of good luck and Godspeed. I shall never forget Jim's farewell. He clasped my hand so firmly it almost broke.

Then with eyes aflame he said, "God go with you, *brother!*"

"God bless you!" I replied, then turned to follow the guard down the hall as the sound of LULU slowly faded from my ears.

I was taken to a good-sized cell with a single plank bed. The cell looked out onto the main courtyard. This was the center of activities and the place where guards and officers lived. My cell was next to the rooms of "Angel-face," the cook and only Vietnamese woman in camp.

I was obviously in a favored place, and I wondered how long it would be until I was free. Then I remembered the list in my sock. I pulled it out and began memorizing with great haste, inventing little devices for remembering each LULU name. After considerable rehearsing, I tore the list into minute scraps and deposited them in my toilet bucket.

The wait began. How soon would I be out? How would I get home? Would I be sent to Russia or Hong Kong? Bill Decker would see me home if I could get to Kowloon, I was sure. A thousand questions flooded my mind, along with an additional thousand suppositions as to how all this would work out.

The lunch hour passed with no sign of food—that was a good indication. With the signing of the treaty, we had all become very sign conscious. Any little suggestion of release was carefully analyzed, along with the vaguest of gestures and variations in diet or camp regulations. These were all interpreted as either good or bad signs. Being so overtly conscious of every little indication bothers me, especially in light of Christ's reply to the Pharisees, "An evil and adulterous generation craves for a sign." One of Les Chopard's favorite verses is, "We walk by faith, not by sight."

145

I sat, seeking for a sign. When a guard happened by, I requested toilet paper, and he returned moments later with three eight-by-twenty-four-inch sheets, equivalent to ten days' ration. I was overjoyed by the luxury. Then I began to wonder, were they being generous, or did it mean I'd be there long enough to use it all? Why this much if I were going to be released in a few hours? One sheet would have been generous. I was deflated. This was a bad omen indeed!

In the afternoon, I was told to bring my chair and sit outside in the sun. The freedom was intoxicating, just to be under the open sky. I peeled down to my briefs and soaked up the warmth. At this point a second sign occurred. My guard disappeared and returned a moment later with a basin of water and a razor, and indicated that I was to shave. I was happy to do so, for this was not one of the usual shave days (Monday or Friday). It could only mean that something special was about to happen and I had to look my best. I shaved carefully, all the time admiring my moustache in the mirror. This was most certainly a good sign. You cannot imagine the anticipation that flowed through me. Two good signs against one bad sign. The odds were improving. When the grooming was complete, I returned to my chair in the sun.

As I worked on my suntan, I happened to notice the camp commandant and his interpreter approaching me. Quickly I pulled on my pajamas and stood at attention, displaying the respect due to his authority.

They asked how I was.

"As well as can be expected, sir."

"Do you know why you have been moved to this section of the camp?"

"No, sir."

It was explained that I had been a very sick man (this was not exactly news, but I'd heard of others in camp who were far more ill) and that it was the desire of the prison authorities that I should be cured. Hence, they would give me extra food, and they wanted me to exercise and sit in the sun.

"Any questions?"

"When am I going home?"

146

"Your case will be considered when the provisional government is set up in Laos," they said, and walked away.

I was crushed. I hated myself for being so gullible, for believing so easily. I didn't want their so-called cure, I wanted to be back with the others. I was choking with frustration.

Shortly after this, I was locked back in my room. I had discovered the real value (both physical and mental) of pacing the floor, and I was doing so when my supper was brought. It was unbelievable. There was a large bowl of soup and a plate of fish the equivalent of a standard ration for ten men. Besides that, there was a loaf of bread, two cans of Bulgarian lunch meat, and a dozen bananas! It was overwhelming. I bowed my head in deep gratitude and prayed that the others might be enjoying a similar banquet.

By the time I had devoured the soup and fish, I was full. But the cans of lunch meat were already opened, so I knew they would not last long. With some effort I polished off one can and a half loaf of bread, saving the rest for a bedtime snack. The food was good, but there was little joy in eating. Why should I get so much when Ernie, who'd been here almost eight years, had never seen grub like this?

I set the leftovers in order and examined the bananas. I counted them over and over, scrutinizing each one carefully to determine which were in poorest shape and should be eaten first.

I paced the floor. Frustrating? Nothing could be more frustrating than this ! After being with others, having the joy of reading the little New Testament with them, I was suddenly cut off. I couldn't stand it! I had some idea by now of what the long hours of solitary were like. Was I to endure them again? Pacing back and forth, I pleaded my case before the Lord. Tomorrow, I told the Lord, I shall beg the authorities to put me back with the other men. I'll forego the extra food and promised freedom. But I won't tolerate solo another night!

In cases such as this, I learned a great deal of the kindness of God. From time to time I found myself fuming away, immersed in self-pity. God never rebuked me, but rather soothed my ruffled spirits and assured me of His love.

I continued to pace and talk with the Lord. Perhaps I could stick it out for more than a day, but I most certainly had to be back with the others for Sunday and the breaking of bread service.

I found a loose nail and wrote out the remaining days until Sunday on the wall. I would scratch off one every day! I set the nail down. Suddenly, sitting there on the end of the bed, I broke. There were no tears; I had passed that point. "Lord, I'm here as long as You want me to be," I said.

After it was dark, I ceased my meditation and lay back on the bed. I was lonely as I'd never been before, and I pray I shall never feel that strong a sense of isolation again. With a heart craving for companionship, I fell asleep.

The next morning I exercised, straightened my bed, and then sat down for a season of prayer. Via the throne of grace I was transported from Hanoi to my home, to my sister in Nigeria, to my church and friends, and then back again. The morning guard told me to pick up my dishes, then led me behind his barracks to the water tanks. The filth and stench were indescribable. He pointed to a concrete tank, where I proceeded to wash my greasy tin plate. Next was a similar tank so full it was threatening to run over into where I was working. I was looking into the second tank when a guard threw in a handful of garbage. It settled to the bottom, next to a large dead rat. I noticed that the animal was intact but its fur was bleached incredibly white. I noticed too that the tank was caked with lime.

In the course of the second day, I was given a large portion of plain sugar, perhaps five pounds. It was considered a real delicacy among prisoners; when sprinkled on bread, the end product tasted remarkably like a glazed donut!

Lunch bore no resemblance to the feast of the previous evening. As I sat in the sun that afternoon, the officer who was second in command brought me seven books and two small cans of powdered milk. He suggested that I read the books and tell him what I thought of them, then he asked if I would need sugar to make up the milk. I said yes, not admitting that I already had more than enough, and received an additional five pounds.

The commandant's translator spent some time with me, quizzing me on political issues concerning the war. I replied with typical vagueness, at times merely grunting, and he looked quite perplexed.

"Is English your native tongue?" he asked.

"Yes, sir."

The books I received were all communist propaganda, and poor propaganda at that. The English was so appalling that it was laughable, bearing a preponderance of long words I'd never even heard. One book was particularly morbid, with detailed descriptions of mutilations and emasculations supposedly perpetrated by enemies of communist freedom fighters. Before I'd read many pages, my spirit revolted and I set the book aside.

The camp doctor paid me a visit, too. According to other prisoners, he was famous for partial extractions and quack prescriptions of every kind. His recommended treatment for one lieutenant colonel suffering from malnutrition was that he should inhale and exhale more often. The patient assured him that he did so frequently! When "Doc" came, he peered at me inquisitively for several moments without comment. I informed him that I still had great difficulty in controlling my bladder and would appreciate some professional assistance.

"More exercise!" was his laconic reply, without any suggestions as to how one exercises the bladder.

By the third day, the extra food had dropped to normal, apart from my carefully-hoarded milk, sugar, and bananas. While I was washing some underclothes in the courtyard that afternoon, an officer came to inform me that my moustache must go—it was against camp rules. I was fully aware of this, but did not want to part with my little project. I intimidated him by telling him that the moustache was an integral part of my culture, and removing it would suggest a degree of cultural genocide on his part. He was taken aback and, not wanting to act like a bourgeoisie, left my "hair lip" to grow.

My rehabilitation was short-lived. On the fourth morning, after some fingerprinting and mug shots, I was returned to LULU. I was a most welcome sight, especially when I unrolled my belongings to reveal the treasure of sugar, books, milk, and five bananas.

That morning ended a total period of twenty-eight days solo, a mere drop in the bucket compared to the years some had spent in confinement. But it deepened my appreciation for human company and reinforced Christ's promise that, "Lo, I am with you alway."

Lovingly,
In the service of
the King of kings,
Lloyd

30

If it had not been the LORD *who was on our side . . . Then the waters would have engulfed us* (Psalm 124:1, 4).

So Lloyd was reunited with the nine. If he were not going to be released, he would rather be with his LULU friends than anywhere else. He learned that they had been in and out of the Snake Pit in a sort of musical cells game for reasons they could not explain, and had managed to collect a few extra bits of furniture in the process.

The uncertainty concerning their time of release was wearing on everyone's nerves. Bets were placed on certain dates—and were lost. According to terms of the treaty, copies of which they now held, they might have to stay for ninety days. Chuck, who had been shot down on the previous Christmas Eve and was the only short-term prisoner in the group, was concerned over the morale of the men; and to stimulate some interest in cell activities, he drew up a plan for a tournament. He signed up everybody for playing games of chess, bridge, and any other sport they could devise. Top winner would earn the title *LULU Tournament Grand Master of 1973*. Games were played with renewed interest.

In addition to the games, Jack, Jim, Lloyd, and Sam began an evening study in the gospel of Luke. One day which came as a welcome break in their routine is described by Sam as "just like a Sunday school picnic!" It was the day Red Cross packages arrived. Once again the commandant, the interpreter, and cameraman were present to record the happy reactions of prisoners receiving wonderful good things in prison. And this time the prisoners actually obliged by smiling! How could they help it when they saw hard candies, butterscotch,

151

books, playing cards, combs, good razor blades, after-shave lotion, and soap? Of potted meat, Vienna sausage, cheese, and crackers, there was just a taste. But what a taste—and a fore-taste of better things to come!

Mid-March they were moved to New Guy Village, which was near the gates and was supposed to be the temporary residence of those destined for release. The new little leaves on the trees in the courtyard symbolized to them the fresh new hopes in their own hearts. Prison regulations were relaxing, and perhaps this was another good sign.

One day when there were noisy crowds on the street outside, a couple of fellows climbed up under the roof and managed to lift the tiles to look out. They saw a bus loading with POWs, and some of the POWs saw them. Fortunately the guards did not. As the bus pulled away, the Lao prisoners raised their voices in "Auld Lang Syne" and "God Bless America," and they thought there was a response. But when would their day come? Chuck found a large smooth plank on which he drew a thermometer and marked the LULU going-home date line—March 14 up to 28. Surely they would be gone by then!

True, there were signs that the day was fast approaching. Guards brought in shoes, pants, shirts, and jackets for fittings, and each person's allotted wardrobe was put into a zippered plastic bag bearing his name and was locked away against the day of his departure. Diet was improving too! Apparently the Vietnamese wanted their prisoners to leave in fairly good physical condition, for there were daily rations of canned meat, and occasionally bananas were brought in.

As March drew to a close, a time was set apart for the special awards assembly as a result of the tournament. The great occasion began seriously, with a speech about the friendship which had deepened between them in prison, and an invocation by Sam. Then the winner and four runners-up stood in the middle of the courtyard in full dress uniform (those cheerful gray prison pajamas). Norm gave a little speech and announced the winner.

It was Lloyd Oppel! Norm placed a crown on Lloyd's head and solemnly presented him with the prize. Cups of tea were raised, and the toast was given. Then four cups of tea immediately doused the winner. Five cups of tea from poor-sport losers doused the runners-up. Dousing which began with tea cups ended with buckets of water; but after all, it was a hot day. In the words of one of the participants, they had "a jolly time!"

On Sunday, March 25, Norm and Chuck came to the service, and both prayed voluntarily. Norm, admittedly skeptical for years, had begun reading the New Testament and entering into some of the Bible discussions. That morning he prayed, "Lord, it says in Your Word, 'blessed are those who have not seen yet have believed.' Lord, help me believe."

There was good singing that morning. Jim had been practicing on his accordion and was managing a few songs fairly well. As they became louder and more enthusiastic in their renditions, a guard came, warning them to be quiet; but they were singing too loudly to understand. "The Battle Hymn of the Republic" really echoed through the halls of the Hanoi Hilton that day.

On March 27, Sam was told to get into his prison pajamas and was then led away to a well-furnished room. He was cordially welcomed by the pleasant man who had been his interrogator during solitary, and another older man. They poured hot bitter tea into tiny cups and served their guest, offering him cookies and nut brittle. After talking for some time, the interrogator came to what appeared to be the reason for the interview.

"When you go home," he said to Sam, "would you be willing to exchange cultural information with us? We would like to send you literature about our country, and to learn about your country and people. Would you do this?"

Sam thought for a moment. Why? What was the reason for the request? Could it have anything to do with what Sam had written on the interrogation papers and his offer to explain more about the Christian faith? If so, he could not refuse.

"Yes, I could do that."

"Would you consider visiting North Vietnam as a tourist?"

Sam hesitated a moment. "Yes, if my plane were to stop here on my way back to Laos."

"Would you consider being a missionary to North Vietnam?"

"Yes," Sam tried not to show his surprise.

"We know missionaries are trying to help the people," the man concluded, "but it is better to stay away from war zones."

After a little more polite talk and pleasantries, Sam rose to leave. When he was offered another cookie, he took advantage of the easy atmosphere and accepted the whole plateful. They seemed surprised, but gave him paper to wrap up his precious loot and take it back to share with his cellmates. Both Lloyd and Sam were called in for several such interviews, some apparently with the hopes of getting statements from them to the effect that they had been well-treated as prisoners of the North Vietnamese. They avoided committing themselves into making positive statements.

That night, there was a feeling of excitement and expectancy among the prisoners from Laos, and also some apprehensions and fears. Some of the men had been in prison for three, four, five—and Ernie, for eight—years. Sleep evaded them, and they were up early on the morning of March 28—the last day on their LULU release thermometer.

31

He sent from above, he took me; he drew me out of many waters; He delivered me from my strong enemy (2 Samuel 22: 17-18).

It was March 28, 1973, early morning, and exactly five months since Lloyd and Sam had hurriedly left their house in the Village in the Jungle by the Troubled Water Lagoon and had been taken prisoners as they drove toward the market in Kengkok.

Suddenly the cell block where the prisoners from Laos were confined was electrified with the news. This is it! They were going to be released!

"Pack your possessions!" Their possessions? How few they were! Lloyd had an old striped T-shirt he'd worn on the trail, still stained with sweat and the persistent jungle rains; a tin cup and spoon; and sandals made from tires. He had his prison uniform which was twice as wide in the hips, twice as long in the crotch, and twice as broad on the shoulders as he needed. He picked up the now worn and frayed New Testament which had brought them such joy. Could he, dare he, slip it into his little bag of possessions? He had asked the guard before if he could take it with him, but had met with a curt refusal. Yet he would try.

They all washed and shaved and changed into the civilian clothes which had been waiting in the plastic bags bearing their names. Then, each clutching his little bag of possessions, the prisoners lined up for inspection. As their senior ranking officer, Walt went through the line first. When it came his turn, Lloyd's heart sank when he noticed the man in charge of checking their possessions—it was the very guard who had told

155

him he could not take the Bible home. Now the guard reached
into Lloyd's bag and came up with the little book in his hand.

"What are you doing with this?"

Lloyd grinned in his most ingratiating manner. "Well, seeing
as this is the last day, I thought you'd be a niće guy and let me
take it home."

"No. I told you! You can't have it."

The little Testament was put to one side, but the incident had
not escaped the watchful eyes of Walt, who had already passed
through the inspection line. He did not believe in God and
could not accept the teachings of the Book, but he had come to
respect Lloyd and Sam, and he knew how much that Testament
meant to them. He waited for his opportunity, and when the
guard was busy in another direction, he walked by the table and
slipped the book under his shirt. Nobody saw him do it.

A scrap of paper from Lloyd's pocket briefly lists that morning's activities:

North Vietnamese look on as Sam Mattix greets the American who came to take the POWs from Hanoi.

Last man out at 8:10 A.M.

Turned over to Lao Patriotic Front at 8:20 A.M.

Reception and turn over at 10:30.

Last man out—all the prisoners had left the notorious Hanoi Hilton by 8:10 that morning. As all the world knew, the prisoners from Laos were the last to be released. Lloyd was not released until the others had gone, and then was turned over to the Lao Patriotic Front who, in turn, were to hand him over to a representative of the Canadian government. Those two hours at the Canadian embassy dragged on.

In the meantime, Sam had gone with the other members of LULU in a transport bus that would take them through Hanoi and to the Gia Lam Airport. He thought Lloyd would be traveling home separately and they would not meet again until somewhere in US or Canada.

The transport bus was delayed for some time at the parking lot, to the distress and mounting concern of its eager-to-get-away occupants. Later they discovered that the delay was because of the wording on the turnover papers: the Americans refused to sign that these were all the POWs from Laos when over three hundred still were unaccounted for.

Finally, the bus pulled up at the doors of a big building. One by one, in order of capture, the prisoners walked from the bus into the terminal for handshakings and picture-takings, and then out to the plane to take their seats. Nine members of the Legendary Union of Laotian Unfortunates were on their way. Today they were the fortunate ones. What of those others who were still missing in action in the jungles of Laos? Then up the ramp came the tenth member of LULU—Lloyd Oppel! There was a cheer.

The T 141 Medic plane began to roll, gained speed, and roared into the sky, leaving nothing but a trail of exhaust to momentarily mark the skies over Hanoi. The men leaned back. They could see the buildings of the great city far below, but they looked up and forward into the clear, clean sky. Up until this moment, they could not really believe it; but they were free, free, free at last! They cheered; they clapped; they whistled. God bless America! Here we come!

Now Lieutenant Colonel Walt reached down into his bag

and pulled out the little Gideon New Testament and solemnly handed it to Lloyd.

"Walt! Thank you, sir!"

They began to talk of the Book and how they had managed to smuggle it away from the guards at the prison.

"Here, what's this all about?" the military photographer aboard wanted to know. So they told the story again.

"Well now, that deserves a picture. Walt, you stand here and hand the book to Lloyd."

"I'll open it to John 3:16, Jack's verse." Lloyd said. "I never thought I'd see the day when the biggest atheist I know was giving me a Bible!"

Walt smiled and looked a little embarrassed. But when he added his autograph to those of the LULU prisoner group on the fly leaf of the Testament he wrote "Complimentary Issue" just over his signature.

At the Clark Air Force base in the Philippines, the men were given medical treatment, good food, and new clothes. Lloyd phoned his parents in Courtenay and told them he was on his way home, and Sam phoned his family in Centralia. Good news—such good news for all their faithful praying friends. But there was sad news too. It was not until Lloyd and Sam met Ken Brooks, missionary in the Philippines, that they heard the fate of the rest of their team. Mr. and Mrs. Chopard had been able to escape, but Beatrice Kosin and Evelyn Anderson had been killed by the North Vietnamese forces which invaded Kengkok.

Sunday, April 1, Lloyd arrived at the McChord airport near Seattle and was met by the commanding officer of the training and rescue squadron of the RCAF at Comox, and flown home.

Home! They were home at last!

Home at last! Lloyd is welcomed by his mother, brother Fred, sister-in-law Audrey, father, and two nephews.

EPILOGUE

Far more than they realized when they started out on the Ho Chi Minh Trail, Lloyd and Sam were called upon to share in many experiences similar to those of the Apostle Paul:

> For we do not want you to be unaware, brethren, of our affliction which came to us in Asia, that we were burdened excessively, beyond our strength, so that we despaired even of life; indeed, we had the sentence of death within ourselves in order that we should not trust in ourselves, but in God who raises the dead; who delivered us from so great a peril of death, and will deliver us, He on whom we have set our hope. And He will yet deliver us, you also joining in helping us through your prayers, that thanks may be given by many persons on our behalf for the favor bestowed upon us through the prayers of many.
>
> 2 CORINTHIANS 1:8-11
> NEW AMERICAN STANDARD BIBLE